Two Beast Fables

Animal Farm

George Orwell

and

The Book of the Dun Cow

Walter Wangerin

Curriculum Unit

Jayne R. Smith

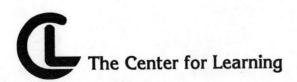
The Center for Learning

Jayne R. Smith, who earned her B.A. and B.F.A. at the University of Oklahoma and M.A. at the University of Texas, has been acclaimed as an English teacher at Jefferson High School, Port Arthur, and also in southwest and national English conferences. She is the author of a number of Center for Learning units, including *Death of a Salesman, Cyrano de Bergerac, The Old Man and the Sea/Ethan Frome, The Martian Chronicles,* and *The Joy Luck Club.*

The Publishing Team

Rose Schaffer, M.A., President/Chief Executive Officer
Bernadette Vetter, M.A., Vice President
Diane Podnar, M.S., Managing Editor
Amy Richards, M.A., Editorial Director

Cover Design

Clare Parfitt

List of credits found on Acknowledgments
Page beginning on 106.

ISBN 1-56077-150-X

Contents

Introduction

Young children love to hear stories about talking animals. The appeal is so basic that it makes best-sellers out of adult fantasy books featuring animals. Sophisticated readers enjoy the layers of meaning, the satire; reluctant readers enjoy the simplicity and the clarity.

This appeal makes George Orwell's *Animal Farm*, a satire about totalitarianism and revolution, and Walter Wangerin's *The Book of the Dun Cow*, a witty and moving parable about the struggle between good and evil, excellent choices for the classroom. Both can be classified as beast fables, a genre popular since Aesop's Fables.

Leonard Biallas, professor and theologian, explains the appeal of beast fables and other myths in this way: "When reason became our goddess, it stifled our imagination. Americans believe there's no problem we can't solve with the proper machine. But what of the questions that telescopes and computers can't answer: Who are we? Why are we here? What happens when we die? For those we want to retain that other thing, those archetypes, those myths."[1]

Animal Farm is an important work for what it says about the inevitability of idealistic revolution turning into a carbon copy of the previous regime. The characters, although affecting, are one-dimensional. It is basically a political book, accessible to all readers.

Dun Cow, like *Animal Farm*, is a book of ideas, but instead of focusing on government, it focuses on people—their strengths, weaknesses, and temptations. It is moral without being didactic and contains much prose that is close to poetry without being cloying. The major animal characters are well-developed and credible. It is accessible to most readers, but its ideas are challenging to the best readers.

Although students of varying levels of reading skills will find this book accessible, its depth of ideas offer challenge to the most skillful readers.

[1]Nancy Shulins, "Keepers of the Flame", *Houston Chronicle*, 26 August 1990, 36.

Teacher Notes

Animal Farm and *The Book of the Dun Cow* have two things in common: both can be called beast fables, and both can be read and appreciated, in differing degrees, at many educational levels from elementary school through college. *Dun Cow*, the lesser known book, won two commendations in 1978 as best youths' book of the year. It also earned the American Book Award for Best Science Fiction in 1980 and was called "a parable for all adults" by *The Christian Science Monitor*. Recently, by popular demand, it was reissued in paperback, along with its sequel *The Book of Sorrows*.

In some schools *Animal Farm* is taught at a lower grade level than *Dun Cow*. The lessons of this unit are arranged so that each book can be taught separately. If both books are studied, the second should not be read until the first has been discussed to some extent. A final handout asks students to compare the two. **Handout 44** offers topics for comparative essay writing.

Answers to handout questions will vary unless otherwise indicated.

Lesson 1 may be used to introduce either or both books. Lesson 5, which introduces *The Book of the Dun Cow*, requires teacher access to "The Nun's Priest's Tale." Lessons 6-9 on *Dun Cow* may be assigned to advanced level students as preliminary work for four panel discussions.

The *Animal Farm* text used for these lessons is the Signet paperback edition, 1946. *The Book of the Dun Cow* text used is the Harper and Row paperback edition, 1989; the page numbers are the same as the Harper and Row hardcover school edition. All references to what the author believes or intended are based on a telephone interview with Mr. Wangerin in August 1990.

Both novels include major aspects not covered to any extent in the lessons of this unit. The study of *Animal Farm* may be enriched by research of Russian history in order to draw parallels. An article in *Time* (February 19, 1990), "Headed for the Dust Heap," is an excellent supplement. In *The Book of the Dun Cow*, medieval aspects of the novel (feudal systems, chivalric lovers, bestiaries, epic elements, etc.) offer opportunities for additional in-depth study of the novel's content.

Supplementary materials include reading quizzes for both novels. For a final test, essay topics may be used.

Students who may be curious about the fate of Mundo Cani Dog and interested in the final adventures of Chaunticleer will enjoy reading the sequel, a moving story.

There is a Beast Fable Society, which holds annual international meetings and which publishes *Bestia* annually. The publication or information is available by sending a stamped, self-addressed envelope to Ben Bennani, Department of Language and Literature, Northeast Missouri State University, Kirksville, MO 63501.

Animal Farm, a seventy-five minute video, is distributed by Hollywood Home Theatre, a division of Budget Video, Inc.

Lesson 1
Beast Fables and All That

Objectives
- To show purpose and use of animal stories
- To introduce terminology

Notes to the Teacher

The four handouts in this lesson can be used as preparation for reading either or both books. Although the lengthy definition in **Handout 3** is from the introduction to *Animal Farm*, it can be readily applied to *The Book of the Dun Cow*.

After students complete **Handout 1**, a delightful story by Saki, "Tobermory," may be assigned or read aloud. Available in many anthologies, it describes what happens when, at a weekend house party, the host's cat suddenly begins to talk and reveals many things he has observed as he strolls unnoticed through the house.

Students should be encouraged to think about why animals are so often used instead of humans in stories, movie cartoons, and comic strips. Is criticism accepted more easily when it is given by or to an animal? Are human foibles more readily enjoyed when ridiculed through animal behavior? Is satire less personally destructive when people are disguised as animals? Readily available comic strips are useful sources for discussion ("Garfield," "Mother Goose and Grimm," "Calvin and Hobbes," "Belvedere," and "Shoe"). Recent reprintings of 1950s "Pogo" strips show how animals can be used to criticize serious social problems such as the McCarthy trials. (Refer to Animal Tale Bibliography for titles.) In the supplementary materials are two handouts to help students in reading and thinking about ideas in *Animal Farm*.

Procedure
1. Distribute **Handout 1**. Discuss the Rover section, the appeal of talking animals and the writer/artist's purpose in using them. The writing assignment may be done individually or in small groups. Ask students to read their dialogues aloud. Can the pet's personality be determined? Is he/she like human beings?

2. Distribute **Handout 2**. Divide the class into six groups. Assign a topic to each group. For further topics for additional groups, use African or Black American animal tales (not Brer Rabbit or Anansi); Arab animal tales (limited resources); or James Thurber's humorous animal fables. Be sure choices include *talking* animals, not merely stories of humans with animals involved. Some sources are listed in the supplementary materials.

3. Distribute **Handout 3** to introduce students to necessary terms and to make them aware of the inadequacy of mere definition for literature purposes. Answers will depend on the selections chosen, though there will likely be no disagreement on Aesop's tale being a fable, it and others may have some qualities that fit other definitions. Although no fairy tale is included in the previous handout since so few have talking animals as main characters, a choice of two familiar ones is given here for analysis. The one they choose may have no miraculous happenings or fantastic transformations, thus not even fitting the definition of a fairy tale.

The Wodehouse definition may be difficult for students. Discuss it with them to be sure they understand his points. Wodehouse gives several examples in the essay in the Signet edition of *Animal Farm*.

Suggested Responses:
1. *Grandma in "Little Red Riding Hood," "Snow White," "Ugly Duckling," etc.*
2. *Some, perhaps, do. There is a moral of some type in many of Andersen's fairy tales and in some of the Grimm tales that have been "softened" by modern retellers like "Little Red Riding Hood."*
3. *"Duckling"—unpleasant things can change; the ugly can become beautiful; people are often cruel to others who are different; what you do will not necessarily make you happier; it was the duckling's natural fate to become a lovely swan.*

"Snow White"—people are cruel without reason; an older person can be jealous of a younger one; parents can harm children. Poison apples represent jealousy.

4. Distribute **Handout 4**.
    Suggested Responses:
    Animal Farm
    1. bossy, arrogant
    2. pure
    3. a leader, a prophet
    4. a "rat," one who tells on others
    5. unimportant
    6. one who whimpers, complains, doesn't fight
    7. a fighter

    The Book of the Dun Cow
    In 9, "Mundo Cani" means "Dog of the World." The evil ones are 8-10-11. John Wesley Weasel's name may confuse students since weasel has bad connotations, yet, John Wesley founded the Methodist Church.

5. Distribute **Handout 5**, which is optional and can be done at any time during the unit. Ask students why the particular animals were chosen and whether they deserve the infamy. Point out that very rarely is an animal word complimentary.
    Suggested Responses:
    1. to copy
    2. to fool around; be curious
    3. to eat too much
    4. to tell on a comrade
    5. to show off
    6. to run around, sometimes in an immoral way
    7. to reduce him to tears or total fear (This word is unfair; it does not come from the animal.)
    8. to play when you should work
    9. to outwit; to fool a clever person
    10. to brag
    11. to follow closely
    12. a long time
    13. to parrot
    14. a. a terrible person ("dirty dog") or, for a girl, ugly
        b. sneaky, dangerous
        c. worthless, a low-life
        d. a coward
        e. a pretty girl
        f. wise or a late-night person
        g. silly
        h. terrible person, dishonest
        i. shy

15. a. dog
    b. dog
    c. fish
    d. fox
    e. eel
    f. owl
    g. bug
    h. bee or beaver
    i. elephant
    j. loon or hyena
    k. lion
    l. sheep
    m. mule

Ask students to think of other uses of animals as words or phrases. As they read *Animal Farm* and *The Book of the Dun Cow*, ask them to observe how the authors use these clichéd ideas about animals.

Talk to the Animals

Directions: Rover has been your pet for many years. He barks and runs in circles when he sees you coming home; he fetches your slippers; he wags his tail when you pat his head. Occasionally, as he lies by your feet in the evening, he looks up at you in adoration. You are his master, he is your willing slave.

What would happen if Rover (or your cat) suddenly were given the power of speech? What would he say when you came home? As he fetched your slippers? What is he *really* thinking when he looks up at you? What does he think about your habits, your dress, your worship of the telephone and the television, your grand meals while he gets a dish of kibble? Would he and the cat gossip behind your back? Do they adore you or secretly laugh at you? Would they give you lectures on behavior; on your treatment of them? Would they be charming or snide? Would you like your pets as much if they could talk?

Write about It

Give your imagination full rein. Write a brief dialogue between a human (you or a fictional person) and a pet (yours or a fictional one) or a dialogue between two pets. Write in play form, establishing first, in your stage directions, what kind of animal is involved and what the setting is. Focus the dialogue on *one* topic (what you feed him, his boring walks, your telephone conversations, etc.). Give the pet a distinct personality. Let him speak conventional English. Choose a serious or humorous approach.

Name _____

Date _____

Animal Tales

Directions: Throughout the history of humanity, people have been fascinated by talking animals. In nearly all such stories, the animals sound suspiciously like humans and behave like humans—from the big bad wolf to Garfield. Some contain morals to tell people how to behave—or how *not* to behave. Others are purely entertaining. Here is your chance to become familiar with some of the various types of animal tales. Your group will be assigned to one of the following topics:

a. an Anansi tale from Africa

b. a Brer Rabbit story

c. an Aesop fable

d. a Mexican folk tale using animals that talk

e. an American Indian myth using animals that talk

f. a very recent children's book using talking animals

Go to the library to select your tale or book. All members of the group should read it or hear it read aloud. Discuss it with your group. Decide on a way to present it to the class other than reading it aloud! Involve all of the group. Let one member compose a brief introduction to your *type* of tale (what is an Anansi tale? Where and how did it develop?). Prepare to make a not more than ten-minute presentation of your story for your class. After your performance, the group will lead the class in a brief discussion of the tale—its moral, its purpose, its effect.

Is a Rose a Rose?

Directions: Read the following definitions from *Benet's Reader's Encyclopedia*, 3rd Ed., Harper & Row, New York, 1987.

Part I

1. *Beast epic* (or beast fable): a tale or collection of tales written in mock epic, allegorical style, in which the central characters are animals and the tone is often satirical. (Mock epic: combines a grand or elevated style with a trivial subject, so that both style and subject matter are burlesqued.)

2. *Allegory*: an extended metaphor in which characters, objects, incidents, or descriptions carry one or more sets of fully developed meanings in addition to their apparent and literal ones. (Examples: a lamb=innocence; a tiger=experience)

3. *Fairy Tales*: having no basis in fact, emphasize miraculous happenings and fantastic transformations.

4. *Fable*: the action of a fable illustrates a moral which is usually (but not always) explicitly stated at the end. . . . [In Aesop's fables] talking animals illustrate human vices, follies, and virtues.

5. *Parable*: a simple story that teaches a lesson or illustrates a moral principle. Like an allegory, details of a parable parallel the details of the situation calling for illustration.

Using the six animal tales you have discussed and a familiar fairy tale, fit each into one of the five categories defined. Classify according to definition.

a. Anansi

b. Brer Rabbit

c. Aesop

d. Mexican tale

e. Indian myth

f. Children's book

g. "The Three Pigs" or "The Ugly Duckling"

Did you have trouble categorizing? Did some fit parts of a definition but not all of it? Did some fit *two* definitions? If so, you have discovered the Great Literary Problem: how to make a work of art fit into a single category. Even Shakespeare's tragedies often do not fit the definition of classical tragedy.

As you read *Animal Farm* and *The Book of the Dun Cow*, you will find that a single label does not neatly fit either one; several will apply to some degree.

C.M. Wodehouse, in his introduction to *Animal Farm*, which the author calls "a fairy story," redefines the label:

> The point about fairy-stories is that they are written not merely without a moral but without a morality. They take place in a world beyond good and evil, where people (or animals) suffer or prosper for reasons unconnected with ethical merit—for being ugly or beautiful respectively, for instance. . . .They never seek to criticize or moralize, to protest or plead or persuade; and if they have an emotional impact on the reader, as the greatest of them do, that is not intrinsic to the stories. . . . The fairy-story that succeeds is in fact not a work of fiction at all. . . . It is a transcription of a view of life into terms of highly simplified symbols; and when it succeeds in its literary purpose, it leaves us with a deep indefinable feeling of truth . . .[1]

Part II

Think about Wodehouse's definition as you read each book. But first answer these questions about the passage:

1. Name two or three fairy tales in which people or animals suffer or prosper for reasons not connected with their being good or bad—or for no reason. An example given by Wodehouse is the young men who try to awaken Sleeping Beauty before the hundred years are up—and die for their failure. Name some others.

2. Wodehouse says fairy tales do not criticize, moralize, persuade, etc. Is he correct? Can you name any that *do* any of these things?

3. "The Ugly Duckling" is obviously a fairy tale that shows a view of life in highly symbolic terms. What is Hans Christian Andersen showing about real life? Does he moralize? What does "Snow White" show about life? What do poison apples represent?

[1]George Orwell, *Animal Farm* (New York: Signet, 1946), x-xi.

Name _____

Date _____

What's in a Name?

Directions: An allegory usually gives characters names that suggest their qualities. The names are sometimes quite obvious: Faith, Temptation, Greed. Sometimes they are more subtle: Goodman Brown, Beelzy (as in Beelzebub), Simon (as in Simon Peter).

What qualities seem to be suggested by these character names in *Animal Farm?*

1. Napoleon

2. Snowball

3. Moses

4. Squealer

5. Minimus

6. Mr. Whymper

7. Boxer

Judging by only their names, which of these characters from *The Book of the Dun Cow* would you expect to represent good? evil?

8. Cockatrice

9. Mundo Cani Dog

10. Toad

11. Ebenezer Rat

12. Lord Russel

13. Chaunticleer

14. the Dun Cow

15. John Wesley Weasel

16. Beryl

It's a Zoo Out There!

Directions: The English language has appropriated the names of numerous animals for common verbs, adjectives, and nouns with very different meanings. See how well you know your animals.

Part A

Can you define these verbs or verb phrases?

  1. to *ape* someone

  2. to *monkey* around

  3. to *pig* out

  4. to *rat* on someone

  5. to *swan* around

  6. to *cat* about

  7. to *cow* someone

  8. to *horse* around

  9. to *outfox* someone

10. to *crow* about something

11. to *dog* someone's footsteps

Part B

Can you answer these questions?

12. "I haven't seen you in a coon's age!" How long is a coon's age?

13. What other creature is also a verb meaning roughly the same as "to ape"?

14. What are you saying about someone when you call him or her one of these names?

    a. dog

    b. viper

    c. skunk

    d. chicken

    e. chick

    f. owl

    g. goose

    h. rat

    i. mousy

15. Complete these clichés with an animal's name:

    a. lazy as a _____

    b. work like a _____

    c. swim like a _____

    d. sly as a _____

    e. slippery as an _____

    f. wise as an _____

    g. cute as a _____

    h. busy as a _____

    i. a memory like an _____

    j. laugh like a _____

    k. roar like a _____

    l. follow like _____

    m. stubborn as a _____

Lesson 2
Revolution

Objectives
- To provide a general background on revolution
- To point out Orwell's purpose in *Animal Farm*
- To develop awareness

Notes to the Teacher

It is possible to analyze Orwell's book as a description of the Russian Revolution: Old Major is Lenin or Marx; Napoleon is Stalin; Snowball is Trotsky, etc. However, this approach detracts from the book's major purpose for Orwell is talking about revolutions and about bad leaders, not a specific event in history. To limit the content to the Russian Revolution is to limit his more comprehensive comment and to make the book merely a clever allegory.

However, some students may like to make such an analysis. A brief summary of the Russian Revolution from 1898 to the present can be found in an article entitled "Headed for the Dustheap" in *Time*, Feb. 19, 1990, which points out how one revolution evolved and how power was misused.

Procedure

1. Distribute **Handout 6**. Discuss the quotations. Ask students to chose *one* to respond to in writing. Apply it to *Animal Farm* or to revolutions in general.

2. Distribute **Handout 7**. Ask students to name characters for each label. Point out that the categories fit many revolutions, from Ireland to Iran.
   Suggested Responses:
   Leader revolted against: Mr. Jones
   Causes: hunger, mistreatment of animals
   Leader: Snowball
   New leader: Napoleon
   Philosopher: Old Major
   Propagandist: Squealer
   Cynic: Benjamin
   Materialist: Mollie
   Worker: Boxer
   Secret police: dogs
   Public: sheep
   Mother: Clover
   Enemies: Jones, Pilkington, Frederick

Song: "Beasts of England"
Slogan: "All Animals Are Equal" or "Four legs good, two legs bad"
Key battle: Battle of the Cowshed

3. Distribute **Handout 8** which asks students to draw a chart of the revolution's aim and result based on the events in Orwell's *Animal Farm*.
   Suggested Responses:
   1. *A circle would be best. At the end the animals are in the same situation they were at the beginning.*
   2. *He seems to say that revolutions do not cure the problems. Nothing really changes.*
   3. *It is again Manor Farm, showing it will be the same as it was at the start. Manor contains the word man; the pigs are now, in effect, what they used to despise: men.*
   4. *The leaders of the revolution were crueler to their animals than the humans were.*

4. Distribute **Handout 9** which updates *Animal Farm* and asks students to check current newscasts and publications for accounts of revolts, of "Animal Farms."

Name _____

Date _____

Writers on Revolution

Directions: Discuss the quotes. Choose one. Write an essay applying it to *Animal Farm*.

1. Camus—Every revolutionary ends up by becoming either an oppressor or a heretic.

2. Bierce—Revolution, *n*.: in politics, an abrupt change in the form of misgovernment.

3. Berrigan—A revolution is interesting insofar as it avoids like the plague the plague it promised to heal.

4. Shaw—Revolutions have never lightened the burden of tyranny, they have only shifted it to another shoulder.

5. Conrad—The scrupulous and the just, the noble, humane and devoted natures, the unselfish and the intelligent, may begin a movement—but it passes away from them. They are not the leaders of revolution. They are its victims.

Revolt of the Animals

Directions: The revolt of the animals in followed conventional revolutionary patterns and included types of "people" inevitably involved. Fill in the blanks below for this summary of the revolution.

Leader revolted against:

Causes:

Leader of revolution:

Despotic new leader:

Philosopher:

Propagandist:

Cynic:

Materialist:

Devoted but ignorant worker:

Secret police:

Ignorant public:

Mother figure:

Enemies:

Revolutionary song:

Revolutionary slogan:

Key battle:

The Revolution Revolves

Directions: Examine this partial list of events following the revolutions.

turning Snowball into a villain

Napoleon's claiming authorship of Snowball's ideas

training the pups

changing the slogan

changing the commandments

trading with the enemy

pigs sleeping in beds

killing citizens who confess to imaginary crimes

increase in work/no increase in reward

food shortages

Napoleon's honors and medals

Napoleon's drinking

Squealer's "explanations"

Boxer's removal

the dinner with humans

the change in the pigs' appearance

A revolution's aim is progress for the people, the common men. A chart showing its intended direction and result would look like this:

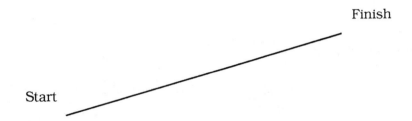

1. Considering the events listed above, draw a chart for the animals' situation, from start to finish.

2. What point is Orwell making by these events.

3. What significance is there in the name change of the farm at the end?

4. At the banquet at the end of the novel, Mr. Pilkington says in praise of *Animal Farm*, " The lower animals did more work and received less food than any animals in the country" and he and the other farmers intend to copy many features of the farm. What point is Orwell making?

After the Revolution

Directions: Because of the terrible social situation Orwell showed in *1984*, people and even governments dreaded the approach of the year 1984. But the year passed without the conditions pictured in the novel.

But 1989 proved to be the year that would make Orwell smile, for many totalitarian "animal farms" revolted from communist control: Hungary, Romania, East Germany, Czechoslovakia, parts of the U.S.S.R., Armenia, Latvia, Lithuania, and Georgia.

- In Romania, where President Ceausescu was destroying ethnic villages and banning typewriters, he and his wife were killed and a new government—ostensibly better—was installed.

- Hungary became the place where freedom-seekers came. It removed the big red neon stars from the tops of its buildings.

- East Germany tore down the infamous Berlin Wall.

- A playwright, who had earlier been imprisoned for his political beliefs, became president of Czechoslovakia.

- The Russian Central Committee voted to give up some of the luxuries they, like the pigs, had been allowed: gourmet food (instead of potatoes and porridge), limousines, fancy apartments.

- Russian newspapers printed criticisms of the government.

These were bloodless revolutions, sanctioned by Chairman Gorbachev. People soon learned that their problems were not at an end. Factories could not afford modern equipment to make well-made cars and appliances at affordable prices. Money was of no value if there was no food to buy. Refugees could not find jobs or homes. They faced a high price to pay for freedom.

Check your daily newscast, newspaper, and weekly news magazines. What is the current situation in Eastern European countries? In Baltic countries? In the Soviet satellite countries? Have the new revolutions succeeded? Are other countries revolting? Jot down notes for a class discussion. Are there any parallels to *Animal Farm?*

How Times Change: A Footnote

Animal Farm—"All that is not forbidden is compulsory."

East Germany, July 1990—A police officer, commenting on a loud sound truck:
"It's not illegal. Nowadays, all that is not prohibited is permitted."[1]

---

[1]*Time*, 30 July 1990, 31.

Lesson 3
Manipulating Minds

Objectives
- To become aware of Doublespeak
- To recognize how language can be used to manipulate people

Notes to the Teacher

Although the manipulation of language is not as significant in *Animal Farm* as it is in *1984*, it is an important aspect of the book. Students need to understand how Napoleon and Squealer controlled the animal's minds and actions through propaganda.

As the use of propaganda in the novel is discussed, students should note the animals' reactions to the changes in the slogans: their memory of a difference and their immediate acceptance of the "fact" that the slogan had always been as it was now. Napoleon uses language to turn them against Snowball; Squealer explains to them that poor Boxer died in the hospital; Boxer, ever loyal to the cause, believes everything Napoleon says. The animals are even convinced that the battle in which the windmill was destroyed was a glorious victory.

The material on Doublespeak is from the N.C.T.E. Committee on Doublespeak and is available from William Lutz, Rutgers University, Camden, N.J. 08102 or from the National Council of Teachers of English. Ask for "Some Examples of Doublespeak" and "Recipients of the Doublespeak Award." These give many more excellent (and often frightening) examples.

Procedure

1. Distribute **Handout 10** to be done individually or in class. Discuss the Orwell quotation. If you prefer, you can go directly to **Handout 12**, the exercise on writing Doublespeak, instead of doing it after **Handout 10**.
   Suggested Responses:
   1. *used car*
   2. *firing people*
   3. *fired*
   4. *undertaker*
   5. *employee theft*
   6. *re-run*
   7. *desk*
   8. *sports*
   9. *learning*
   10. *test*
   11. *taxi driver*
   12. *solitary confinement*
   13. *unlawful*
   14. *sidewalks*
   15. *dying*
   16. *bombing*
   17. *kill*
   18. *bombs that fall on schools, etc.*
   19. *bombing*
   20. *pencil (Army-style)*

2. Distribute **Handout 11** to be done individually or in small groups. The song "Beasts of England" is probably loosely based on Shelley's 1819 poem, "Song to the Men of England."
   Suggested Responses:
   1. *Equal cannot be modified by such words as more or less; an impossible statement.*
   2. *It destroys the original commandment.*
   3. *It keeps them from being commandments; idealism is lost.*
   4. *"Beasts of England" shows the Utopian dream—freedom from harness and whips, plenty of food, perfection. It describes a Sugarcandy Mountain, such as Moses speaks of, but his is for after death. The song gives hope for all. "Comrade Napoleon," with its line "Lord of the swill-bucket," makes no mention of freedom; it is praising a dictator and giving him credit for everything, including what they do not have, such as "full belly twice a day"; shows that only a few profit from a revolution.*
   5. *They will not expect any freedom or any better conditions.*
   6. *Napoleon awards himself "Animal Hero, First Class," "Animal Hero, Second Class," and The Order of the Green Banner.*

3. Distribute **Handout 12** for students to find examples of propaganda devices in *Animal Farm* and to determine their effectiveness.
   Suggested Responses:
   1. *Snowball is the scapegoat and namecalling is used against him as are appeals to fear and hatred.*

2. *Atrocity Tales are told about the farmers' animals.*

3. *Napoleon is given glittering names and confuses the animals by changing enemies from farmer to farmer, by adjusting slogans, and by converting to a man.*

4. *The pigs are stereotyped as brilliant leaders who need the extra food and cannot take time to do dirty work.*

5. *The animals are described as underdogs as long as that label keeps them slaving away.*

4. Distribute **Handout 13** for students to create propaganda terms through language devices and doublespeak through euphemisms. The handout can be done individually or in groups or can be assigned as homework.

Doublespeak

Directions: In another book also published in 1948, *1984*, Orwell showed how a strong central government can limit and manipulate the language and thus control people's minds. Words that were considered dangerous were removed from the language. A new language, Newspeak, was invented, one with few words. Euphemisms (pleasant words for unpleasant ideas: i.e., perspire for sweat) were used to mislead people. A system called Doublethink was used so that people could accept two contradictory statements as true.

In 1974 the term *doublespeak* was invented, using Orwell's *doublethink* and *newspeak* as its basis. Doublespeak means confusing or deceptive language. It has been found in every profession and occupation from education to advertising to law. But the place where doublespeak proliferates is in government.

After World War II the War Department was renamed the Department of Defense. Can you see the difference?

What do these terms mean?

1. experienced car

2. reduction in force

3. selected out

4. grief therapist

5. inventory shrinkage

6. encore telecast

7. pupil station

8. movement experiences

9. adjusted behavior

10. feedback

11. urban transport specialist

12. individual behavior adjustment unit

13. inappropriate

14. people expressways

15. terminal living

16. protective reaction strike

17. eliminate with extreme prejudice

18. incontinent ordinance

19. air support

20. portable hand-held communication inscriber[1]

Now read this quotation from Orwell's "Politics and the English Language:"

Political language . . . is designed to make lies sound truthful and murder respectable and to give an appearance of solidarity to pure wind.

Do you agree? Why or why not?

[1]"Some Examples of Doublespeak," N.C.T.E. Committee on Doublespeak.

Manipulating Language

"All animals are equal—but some are more equal than others."

Squealer, the master manipulator of animal language, made only a small addition to the noble first commandment: "All animals are equal."

Directions Answer the following questions:

1. In what way is the phrase "more equal" doublespeak?

2. What does the addition do to the original commandment?

3. Other commandments, before they all disappeared, were altered:
   No animal shall kill any other animal *without cause.*
   No animal shall drink alcohol *to excess.*
   No animal shall sleep in a bed *with sheets.*

   In each case a limiting phrase was added. What is the effect of the limiting phrases?

4. Read carefully the words to the revolutionary song "Beasts of England" (chap. 1) and Minimus' poem "Comrade Napoleon" (chap. 8). How do they differ? How does the first one embody the idea of the revolution and the second the result of the revolution?

5. At the end of chapter 7, when the animals mournfully sing "Beasts of England," Squealer tells them the song has been abolished. He says that in the song "we expressed our longing for a better society in days to come. But that society has now been established. Clearly this song has no longer any purpose." What is the more likely reason for this censorship?

6. Russians, before 1989, were told that Leonid Brezhnev won the nation's highest medal during World War II, although the medal was not given to him until he controlled Russia twenty years later. What event in the novel parallels this fact?

Propaganda Down on the Farm

Directions: Study the following examples. Find similar examples in *Animal Farm*.

There are dozens of propaganda devices used by countries or political parties within a country. Here are a few: (The first two examples were used by Hitler in Germany.)

Scapegoat (Jews are evil and responsible for all our troubles)

Over-simplified stereotype (Nazis are supermen)

Appeal to hatred and fear (exaggerated emotional statements)

Namecalling ("America—The Great Satan")

Atrocity story (tales of torture, cruelty, etc.)

Appeal to sympathy for underdog ("We are weak and helpless")

Glittering names ("Savior of the People")

Glittering generalities ("law and order," "The American Way")

Confusion (changes in attitude and/or policies)[1]

Find examples of these techniques in *Animal Farm*. State how effective they are.

[1]Gladys and Marcella Thum, *Persuasion and Propaganda in War and Peace* (Evanston: McDougal, Littel, 1974).

You Too Can Be a Squealer!

Directions: See how easy it is to be a propagandist by merely adding a limiting phrase to a famous commandment or rule.

Add phrases to the following and add some of your own. Use Squealer's revisions as models.

Part A

1. "Do unto others as you would have them do unto you"—

2. "Honor thy father and mother"—

3. "Thou shalt not steal"

4. "Always repay a loan"—

5. "No great deed goes unrewarded"—

6.

7.

8.

Part B Doublespeak

Think of a word or phrase to substitute for each of the words below to ameliorate it. (Examples: garbageman—sanitary engineer; to lie—to misspeak).

9. homework

10. cheat

11. ugly

12. stupid

13. constant talker

14. fail a test

Think of some words that "need" euphemism. Create them.

15.

16.

17.

18.

Lesson 4
Morals and More

Objectives

- To become aware of the symbolic nature of the characters
- To recognize the disintegration of idealism into totalitarianism

Notes to the Teacher

The handouts in this lesson refer students to the earlier lesson on fables and fairy tales, applying the information to the book itself. Questions are intended to cause the student to think about the characters and the meaning of the novel.

The showing of the cartoon version of *Animal Farm* serves as a good introduction to this lesson. If the film is shown, alert students to look for changes made in the movie version and discuss the significance of the changes. Some of the changes include the following:

- Mollie and Clover omitted; Benjamin takes on Clover's role and is not pessimistic.
- The cat is killed; Snowball is shown being killed.
- The song is reduced to "Free, Free, Free."
- Squealer speaks only twice.
- Boxer spouts no slogans, has no retirement dreams does not go to "hospital."
- No medals are awarded.
- No "four legs good, two legs better."
- Jones is not allowed to join raid; he alone blows up windmill.
- Pigs who own farms come to dinner, not men.
- Other animals come to farm.
- Animals rebel against pigs, storm the house, win back their freedom.

This lesson includes writing assignments, both analytical and creative, which may also be used for final evaluation.

1. Distribute **Handout 14** for students to complete.
   Suggested Responses:

Opposite	Category
1. Napoleon	good and bad
2. Boxer	uncaring and devoted
3. The pigs; Old Major	workers and non-workers
4. The Cat; Mollie	idealist and uncaring

5. Snowball	the corrupt and the honest
6. Boxer or Clover	pessimist and optimist
7. Napoleon or Squealer	stupid and bright; powerful and weak; leaders and led
8. Squealer or Mollie	
9. Napoleon	
10. student opinion	
11. loyalty, kindness, perseverance	
12. laziness; flattery	
13. willingness to believe and to be led blindly	
14. the secret police	

2. Distribute **Handout 15** for students to complete.
   Suggested Responses:
   1. **Jones**
      drowns old dogs
      takes away eggs and milk
      sells animals
      mistreats animals
      Snowball
      organizes animals
      plans and leads battle
      Napoleon
      uses dogs to control
      debases Snowball
      makes animals work on Sunday
      trades with men
      changes commandments
      starves hens
      executes "traitors"
   2. Snowball
   3. Napoleon and Jones
   4. Snowball
   5. A revolution never fully favors the "common man." The new leaders will be just like the old.
   6. With it the farm would be comfortable, work would be reduced, and the animals would be truly happy. Without it, they would still be slaves.
   7. He was lazy, helpless, but clever; needed strong-arm enforcers when he turned against idealism.
   8. They accepted—and repeated—what Napoleon and Squealer said and were the most numerous; they were his followers who could outbleat the doubters.
   9. It was for Napoleon to show his power and to create a reign of fear and terror.

3. Distribute **Handout 16** for students to complete.

Suggested Responses:

2. *The reader considers some characters good and some evil, but on the farm the two words were not mentioned or even considered. Animals did not think about right or wrong except when Boxer was being taken away.*

3. a. *Boxer, Snowball, the animals who confess*

   b. *Napoleon, Squealer, Mollie*

5. *Since man cannot change his nature, his world cannot improve. All attempts at reform are doomed.*

6. *The movie eliminates Orwell's pessimistic viewpoint and says that good will prevail. Orwell says evil will prevail. Some viewers and readers consider the ending ambiguous, perhaps suggesting that revolution is cyclical. Perhaps Orwell himself may not have been wholly pessimistic since he suggests that man has the impetus to revolt against evil and the ability to imagine a better world. His writing of* Animal Farm *might be called an act of faith, a belief that conditions can be improved.*

4. Distribute **Handout 17** for students to choose writing assignments as directed by the teacher.

Lord of the Swill Bucket

Directions:

Part A

In a beast fable, fairy tale, allegory, or myth, the characters are not fully developed, since they represent qualities and are not intended as real people.

The characters in Orwell's *Animal Farm* can be divided into various categories: the good and the bad; the powerful and the weak; the honest and the corrupt; the workers and the non-workers; the leaders and the led; the pessimists and the optimists; the idealists and the pragmatists; the stupid and the bright.

Determine which character is the opposite of each of the characters listed below and which category states the difference. Be prepared to defend your choices.

	Opposite	Category
1. Snowball		
2. Mollie		
3. Boxer		
4. Clover		
5. Mr. Jones		
6. Benjamin		
7. The sheep		

Part B

Answer the following questions:

8. Which animal is most like Mr. Whymper?

9. Which animal is most like Mr. Jones?

Name _____

Date _____

10. Which two animals do you admire the most? What are their good qualities? How do they differ?

11. What common qualities in mankind does Mollie represent?

12. What human qualities does Moses, the raven, have?

13. What quality do the sheep have that traditionally the masses of people have?

14. In a totalitarian society, who would the dogs represent?

The Power and the Glory

Directions: Although Old Major based his philosophy on idealism, that idealism soon turned to a quest for power. *Animal Farm* is about power and the use and abuse of power. The farm characters who use power in different ways are named below. Under each name, list examples of the character's actions, good or bad, that show his power, and answer the questions that follow.

1.

Jones	Snowball	Napoleon

2. Which of the three uses power for good or positive reasons?

3. Which of the three uses it for bad or negative reasons?

4. Which one is turned into a scapegoat, held responsible for all that goes wrong?

5. From the beginning of the revolution, the pigs, who held the power, did not work. What is Orwell inferring by this fact?

6. In what sense is the windmill a symbol of power?

7. Why were the dogs necessary for Napoleon?

8. Why were the sheep necessary?

9. Why was it necessary for the animals to confess their imaginary or real sins and to be publicly killed?

10. Must a leader, in order to use his power properly, use violence? Why or why not?

11. Lord Acton said, "Power corrupts. Absolute power corrupts absolutely." How does Orwell's novel prove that statement?

Return to the Fairy Tale

Directions: Refer to Wodehouse's definition of a fairy tale. Apply it to *Animal Farm,* and respond to the following questions.

1. "[Fairy-stories] are written not merely without a moral but without morality."

    a. Can you find any moral in the novel? If so, what is it?

    b. Which characters apparently lack morality?

2. "They take place in a world beyond good and evil, ..." Why is the world of *Animal Farm* beyond good and evil?

3. ". . . where people (or animals) suffer or prosper for reasons unconnected with ethical merit . . ."

    a. Which characters suffer even though they do no evil?

    b. Which characters prosper even though they *do* evil?

4. "They never seek to criticize or moralize, to protest or plead or persuade . . ."

    Although the story in itself does not do these things, it does often make an emotional impact or arouses protest. How did you react to the following incidents?

    a. Napoleon's treatment of Snowball

    b. The sheep bleating "Four legs good, two legs *better!*"

    c. The slaughtering of the hens and the others

d. The destruction of the windmill

e. Boxer's hard work despite age and injury

f. Boxer's believing Napoleon about the battle

g. The selling of Boxer to the slaughterer

h. The pigs' socializing with humans

i. The pigs' walking on two legs

5. Why do you suppose Orwell refused to end his fairy tale with "and they all lived happily ever after?" What point does he make with his unhappy ending?

6. If you saw the movie version, why do you think the producers changed the ending? How does the change affect Orwell's story?

Writing about Animal Farm

1. Discuss Napoleon as an example of someone corrupted by power.

2. In *Animal Farm*, Squealer is the propagandist. Using at least three scenes, show how his ability to use language well affects the events in the novel.

3. Using Boxer and the sheep as your prime examples, explain why an intelligent, educated populace is necessary for a good government to work (or show how an uneducated citizenry can enable a bad government to succeed).

4. Compare Snowball and Napoleon as leaders.

5. Choose three minor characters (Mollie, Benjamin, The Cat, Old Major, Clover). Discuss the role of each in the novel.

6. The novel can be viewed as a warning. About what specific types of dangers might Orwell be warning his readers? What specific events in the book prove your points?

7. Beginning with the initial disappearance of the milk, trace the clues that show the pigs, like many revolutionaries before them, are gradually becoming just like those they overthrew and denounced.

8. Discuss Snowball as Napoleon's scapegoat. Why was he blamed for so many things? Why was his history rewritten?

9. Find parallels between *Animal Farm* and events in any totalitarian country. Point out and explain these parallels.

10. You are Clover. Following Boxer's death, you secretly gather the younger animals who had known him only as an old horse and tell them why Boxer was worthy of their praise. Write this as a speech.

11. The novel satirizes many aspects of our society and many types of people. Discuss the novel as a satire.

12. Choose two or three animals with which you are most sympathetic and explain why. Tell what type of *person* each animal represents.

13. Using only the novel, determine George Orwell's political philosophy. Support your decision through references to events in the novel.

14. Become an Orwell. Choose one *specific* flaw in your country, city, school, etc. Write a paper explaining what the flaw is, why it must be corrected, and how it is to be corrected.

15. Be creative. Choose one *specific* flaw in your country, city, school, etc. Write a satire—with or without animals—that clearly reveals this flaw humorously.

16. Decide on a common character flaw: jealousy, a tendency to show off, dishonesty, etc. Choose a suitable animal to represent this flaw, and write a brief scene which both describes and shows it in action.

17. Create an Animal School. Choose at least three or four school types and decide on animals to represent each. Write a satire in which they reveal the kind of people they are.

Lesson 5
Introducing *The Book of the Dun Cow*

Objective
- To provide necessary background for reading the novel

Notes to the Teacher
The Book of the Dun Cow, although often compared to *Animal Farm*, *Watership Down*, and other fantasies, is unlike them in that it contains no human characters and is humorous. Despite the dominance of humor, intermingled are dramatic elements of tragedy. The characters of God and Wyrm lift it to the level of the tragedy of man.

The use of Chaucer's *The Nun's Priest's Tale* is necessary to make Wangerin's characters recognizable and to let students see how an author uses a source. The questions provided prepare them for Wangerin's adaptations and for his allegories and dream sequences. "Chanticleer" and "Chaunticleer" are merely alternate versions of the same name; for consistency, the latter is used in discussing both. In addition, students might enjoy animator Don Bluth's new adaptation of Chaucer's story, "Rock-a-Doodle."

Although the story takes place, like fairy tales, at no defined place or time—once upon a time in a land far away—Wangerin uses many characters, terms, and conventions from medieval literature. Not all of them will be discussed in these lessons, but students need to be aware of some of them.

Handout 21 may be distributed *before* students read the book and discussed later. A quiz on minor characters is included in the supplementary materials. Reading aloud chapter 1 to students will initiate them into Wangerin's humor and encourage discussion as to his choice of style and tone.

Procedure
1. Provide for in-class reading of "The Nun's Priest's Tale." Copies of the poem may be distributed with separate sections assigned to capable student readers. If available, a modern English recording of "The Nun's Priest's Tale" may be used instead of or in conjunction with the printed version.

2. Distribute **Handout 18**. Ask students to respond to the questions.
   Suggested Responses:
   1. *proud, easily convinced, easily flattered*
   2. *sure of herself, good at medicine, bossy*
   3. *clever, smug, tricky, proud*
   4. *Chaunticleer's dream was accurate but Pertelote calls him a coward for believing in dreams.*
   5. *The Fox outwits Chaunticleer and then is outfoxed by Chaunticleer.*
   6. *Chaunticleer's pride makes him ignore the dream and believe the Fox; the Fox's pride makes him fall for Chaunticleer's trick.*
   7. *Do not fall for flattery. Do not blink instead of looking. Hold your tongue.*
   8. *It is satirical, uses animals, and has much epic formality.*
   9. *They suggest that in dreams we learn the truth.*
   10. *Chaunticleer: pride*
       Russell: flattery; sneakiness
       Pertelote: Smugness(?), certainty
   11. *Although he is too proud and too easily flattered and swayed, he shows himself to be clever, and he does learn his lesson.*
   12. *Not very—he is sneaky, treacherous, and easily flattered*

3. Distribute **Handout 19** for students to read the source story of the "Dun Cow."
   Suggested Responses:
   1. *The Dun Cow's functions are to soothe those who are upset, to show compassion, to absorb others' suffering, to inspire others, to heal, and to sacrifice.*
   2. *She can represent the Holy Spirit or an angel.*

4. Distribute **Handout 20** for students to peruse and answer questions.
   Suggested Responses:
   1. *prime—wake-up*
      lauds—start work
      lauds to none—what kind of day it is
      vespers—stop work, eat, rest
      compline—rest and sleep; you are safe
   2. *warnings, joy, grief, shame, death, pride, just for the fun of it*

3. *cruel, sharp, explosive, murderous, thwarting*
4. *He forgot them or did them at the wrong times.*
5. *They drive back the Basilisks; they give courage to his animals.*

5. Distribute **Handout 21**, a reading guide. As evaluation, use the quiz in the supplementary materials, allowing students to use their "minors" sheets.

Name _____

Date _____

Chaucer's Chaunticleer

Directions: Notice these characters and elements which Wangerin uses or adapts in his novel. Write a brief characterization of each character and a brief description of the elements *or* where they occur.

1. Chaunticleer

2. Pertelote

3. Lord Russell

4. interpretation of dreams

5. reversal of fortune

6. pride

7. What is the moral of Chaucer's story?

8. In what ways does it (or does it not) fit the definition of a beast epic given in Lesson 3?

9. What is the importance of the dreams in the story?

10. What characteristics of humans (in an allegorical sense) does each of the three characters represent?

11. How admirable a "person" is Chaunticleer?

12. How admirable is the fox?

Holy Cow!

Directions: Read the legend (source) of the *Dun Cow*.

Once upon a time in England, on a small island called Lindisfarne, lived in a monastery a saint named Cuthbert. The ruins of this monastery still stand. Cuthbert asked his fellow monks to take his body from the Holy Island if they ever left, never to return. In 875, when the Vikings returned for a second attack, the monks took St. Cuthbert's body and crossed to the mainland. More than a hundred years later the monks of the order decided to return the casket to Lindisfarne.

As they walked, the casket suddenly became very heavy and could not be carried further. A few days later a monk had a vision in which he was told to take the body to Dunholme. Unfortunately no one knew where that was.

However, they soon heard two milkmaids talking. One said she had lost her cow. The other replied, "I saw it at Dunholme." The monks then picked up the now light casket and followed the milkmaids to Dunholme, now called Durham, where they found the dun cow, buried St. Cuthbert, and built the first Durham Cathedral over his body.

If you visit Durham Cathedral today, you will find the Street of the Dun Cow and the House of the Dun Cow immediately behind the cathedral. High on the front of the enormous cathedral is the carving of the Dun Cow and the two maidens.

This is the alleged source of the book's name—a cow that served as a messenger from God for the monks. However, the actual source is a Celtic book, dating from 1100 A.D., that was bound in brown (*dun*) cowhide and thus was referred to as the Book of the Dun Cow. It is a collection of unexciting essays whose title alone appealed to the writer of this novel.

As you read the book, pay careful attention to the Dun Cow, who appears only occasionally and rarely speaks but is very important to those to whom she appears. She is mentioned twice before she appears.

1. What are her functions?

2. What might she represent?

Sources: Local History Cards #271. Gatehouse Prints. "From Lindisfarne to Durham," Marygate House, 1980 (Berwick, England: Howe and Blackhall Printers, 7553).

I Gotta Crow!

Directions: *The Book of the Dun Cow* contains many medieval characteristics—a courtly romance, a Chaucerian tale, mythical beasts, dream visions, knightly rescues of maidens and fighting of foes, and a lord of the manor (or rather of a Coop), who protects all the "people" of his land.

In this novel, however, the lord is a Rooster who has to crow to keep order in his land. His crows are of three types: occasional, canonical, and Crows Potens. The canonical crows are the times the bells were rung in medieval monasteries announcing the hours for prayers, chapel, etc. Chaunticleer's canonical crows bear the same medieval terms:

prime   —   dawn

lauds   —   just after dawn

terce   —   three hours later

sext   —   six hours later

vespers   —   sundown

compline   —   nightfall

1. As you read, keep track of Chaunticleer's crows and their purposes.

prime   —

lauds   —

terce   —

sext   —

vespers   —

compline   —

2. List some occasions for his occasional crows.

3. Define *Crows Potens.*

4. What went wrong with Senex's crows?

5. How were Chaunticleer's crows used in battle?

Name _____

Date _____

A Reading Guide
The Minors

Directions: As you read, fill in this chart featuring the minor characters, animals who do not play a leading role but who are important in the novel.

Character	Description	Key Actions
ex: Mundo Cani Dog	big nose, weeps, obeys, runs like wind, hates himself	rescues mice, turkeys, Weasel; fights Wyrm
John Wesley Weasel		
Lord Russel		
Beryl		
Ebenezer Rat		
Wee Widow Mouse		
Pins 1, 5, and 10		
Cockatrice		
Basilisks		
Toad		
Mouse		
Wyrm		
Tick Tock Ant		
Scrape Otter		
Senex		
Ocellata Turkey		
Scarce Mosquito		
the Deer Nimbus		
the Ants		
the Bees		

Also, always pay *close* attention to the major characters: Chaunticleer, Pertelote, and Mundo Cani Dog.

Lesson 6

The Keepers and the Kept

Objectives

- To introduce a simplified version of medieval thought
- To comprehend the characteristics of each of the animals

Notes to the Teacher

Wangerin presents a medieval view in his book complete with cosmography, mythical creatures, courtly figures, and feudalistic society with lords and loyal vassals. As a medievalist, he took pleasure in the accuracy of his parallel world, but the novel does not require deep understanding of the medieval world to follow his story.

Wangerin's major characters are *not* mere symbols but fully developed characters with strengths and weaknesses. He develops, to varying extent, some of the minor characters, mainly John Wesley Weasel, Beryl, and Wee Widow Mouse. But even Ebenezer Rat is excused and redeemed. Chaunticleer must lecture John for accusing Ebenezer of the Pins' death: "I should become a rat to kill a Rat! Avenge revenge? Why, that's sin." And the Rat dies killing a serpent. A small mouse proves to be an unlikely hero against large foes.

Names of minor characters are of interest. All of the hens (except Pertelote) are named for gemstones, the turkey, except for Ocellata, have names referring to food; Ocellata is "spotted turkey;" Thuringer is a sausage; Senex is a foolish, vain old man in ancient comedies; a nimbus is a halo. Wangerin used *Pins* to suggest three things: bowling pins (numbered 1, 5, and 10) which can be easily knocked down; safety pins, which are small and sharp; and pinions (feathers). He created the creature Wyrm, combining the serpent in the garden with Loki, the Scandinavian folk monster, and the Egyptian serpent always pictured with his tail in his mouth. Many medieval travelers took weasels with them as protection from Basilisks.

The fact that his Dun Cow resembles the cow in the St. Cuthbert story is one of many coincidences in his writing of the book.

Procedure

1. Distribute **Handout 22** for students to read and to answer the ensuing questions.
   Suggested Responses:
   1. *the animals*
   2. *messenger from God*
   3. *He stretched around the earth.*
   4. *the scraping off of his skin*
   5. *God had imprisoned him.*
   6. *They were inferior to him.*
   7. *"Whirling—wild, helpless and ignorant—among the blind stars"*
   8. *The order the universe once had is no longer present. The beauty and awe are often missing also. We have walked on the moon and put machines on Mars. We have substituted scientific knowledge for medieval order.*

2. Distribute **Handout 23** for students to read about Basilisks and to answer the questions.
   Suggested Responses:
   1. *1, 2, 3, 4, 5, 12 (perhaps 7)*
   2. *8, 9*
   3. *6—The plot would end if his looks could kill.*
      10—Black suggests evil.
      11—A desert would be out of place in the story.
   4. a. *was imprisoned underground*
      b. *was enormous—could wrap around earth and bite its own tail*
      c. *could crawl through dirt*
      d. *stank fearfully (outer skin always rotting)*
      e. *was lonely, powerful, evil, and angry*
      f. *hated God*
   5. *We consider worms beneath us, lowly. They crawl in the earth; they are miniature serpents.*
   6. *The Serpent*
   7. *To tempt him, as the Serpent does Eve*

3. Distribute **Handout 24** for students to complete.

Suggested Responses:

Chaunticleer	Mundo Cani
rescues Pertelote	saves mice
rescues Wee Widow Mouse	puts nose in hole
deals with tragedy	saves turkeys
confesses his sins	rescues John
gives animals confidence	brings Chaunticleer back
crows during battle	to his senses
defeats Cockatrice	fights Wyrm

John Wesley	Pertelote
mourns Wee Widow	dares to trick Cockatrice
fights Basilisks	sings to the animals
	gives Chaunticleer faith
	brings Chaunticleer and John
	Wesley out of their
	depression

2. tricking Cockatrice; singing to animals
3. giving Chaunticleer faith in the forest; fighting their depression
4. Yes—she has no weapons or strength.
5. Both animals had given up: John Wesley to his anger and grief, Chaunticleer to his jealousy and hatred of Mundo Cani for being the one to fight Wyrm. She made them admit their flaws and brought them back to life, arguing with each other over who will go to the Underworld.
6. She is not a believer in folk medicine. (Beryl is.) She does not boss Chaunticleer although she does persuade him at times. First, helpless in her fear, she is later strong despite her fear. She lacks the certainty of Chaucer's Pertelote; far more likeable and admirable.

4. Distribute **Handout 25**.

5. Distribute **Handout 26**. Assign small groups for discussion with special focus on the Turkeys' characteristics, their likeness to human beings. Share group results with the class.

Medieval Cosmography

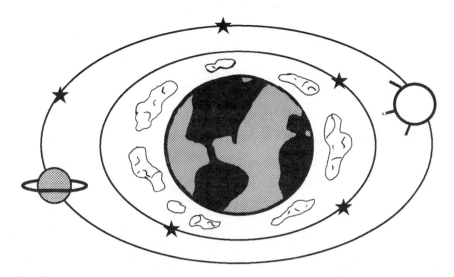

Directions: Read the following information and answer the questions.

Here is the world as many people in the Medieval Age saw it, with sun, stars and planets revolving around the earth which stood still. Halfway between earth and stars floated the clouds and, as Wangerin says, "God still chose to walk among the clouds, striding, like a man who strides through his garden in the sweet evening."

To the people, this concept seemed logical and understandable. The world was not full of unanswerable questions. The moon was an exciting, unreachable place. The stars were things to wish upon.

The 18th-century poet William Blake, in his poem "Tyger," speaks of the stars as medieval people saw them:

> When the stars threw down their spears,
> Watering Heaven with their tears,
> Did He smile His work to see?
> Did He who make the lamb make thee?

People in earlier times could take the first two lines of this stanza literally. Stars *could* throw spears—why not? (In much religious poetry, *stars*, *host*, and *angels* are interchangeable words—as in "a heavenly host." In this poem, the stars represent the angels who fell with Satan from Heaven.)

Everything has an order and its place. The place for Evil was deep under the earth. Evil was, of course, in the shape of a serpent—an angry, smelly, powerful serpent. The animals were the Keepers.

The world had three levels:

> God
> Earth
> Evil

Earth was the battlefield for the constant war between God and Evil.

Wangerin describes the cosmography (literally "a written world") in chapter 4. Jot down the answers to these questions to establish some key facts about the world.

1. Who were the keepers?

2. What was the Dun Cow's function?

3. How big was Wyrm?

4. Why did he smell?

5. Why did he hate God?

6. How did Wyrm feel about his Keepers?

7. Early in the chapter, how does the author describe the earth now, when it is no longer firmly glued in place at the center of the universe?

8. What does his description suggest?

Mythical Monsters

Directions: Read the following information and answer the questions.

Seen any basilisks lately? Is there a Cockatrice in your backyard? Are they hobnobbing with their other mythical friends the Unicorns and the Griffins, the Centaurs and the Dragons?

Basilisks were described as early as 77 A.D. by the Latin writer Pliny. As legends about them increased, more qualities were attributed to them and, in a confusion of language twists, the word "cockatrice," which means the same thing as "basilisk," was sometimes taken to describe a somewhat different animal. Their characteristics were so intertwined by the time of Medieval Bestiaries (books describing supposedly real animals) that they are inseparable.

Fig. 6.1

Here are the descriptions of a Basilisk/Cockatrice:

1. Comes from the egg of an elderly cock

2. Is hatched by a toad

3. Has the upper body of a rooster and the lower body of a snake

4. Has an erect head like a cobra

5. Can kill with its smell

6. Can kill with its look

7. Can kill with its hisses

8. Can be conquered by weasels

Fig. 6.1. White, *The Bestiary*, 168.

Name _____
Date _____

9. Can be killed by a rooster's crow

10. Is striped lengthwise

11. Rules over a desert

12. Is the king of serpents

Sources: Lawrence A. Reiner, "The Baselisks," *Mythical and Fabulous Creatures*, Malcolm South, ed. (Westport, Colo.: Greenwood Press, 1987), 113-119.

T.H. White, *The Bestiary: A Book of Beasts* (N.Y.: J.P. Putnam's Press, 1960), 168-169.

1. Which of these qualities fit Wangerin's Cockatrice?

2. Which fit the Basilisks?

3. List the unused qualities and tell why you think Wangerin chose *not* to use them.

4. Although ancient Bestiaries described many types of worms, they did not describe Wyrm, a creation of the author. Near the end of the book, we learn he has one eye. Using chapter 4, list the other facts that describe Wyrm.

    a.

    b.

    c.

    d.

    e.

    f.

5. Why do you suppose Wangerin chose to make this creature of evil a *worm?*

6. If the Coop symbolizes a king of Eden and Chaunticleer and Pertelote symbolize Adam and Eve, who does Wyrm symbolize?

7. Early in the story when, to Chaunticleer, Wyrm is merely a voice, what does Wyrm try to do?

Note: Wrym speaks in Latin, the language of the supernatural. "Sum Wyrm, subterra" means "I am Wyrm, under the earth."

Name _____
Date _____

Heroes: What the World Needs Now

Directions: List heroic actions of the Coop characters named below and answer the questions.

Who are your heroes who are alive today? What makes them heroes? Would many other people agree? Have they lived virtuous lives? Done daring or admirable deeds? Saved other people's lives? Sought to help others? Have they become rich and famous? Sung loudly? Looked glamorous in movies or on TV? Been tough and macho?

What makes a hero? Should he be something more than other people? Should he take risks for others? Should he be someone you envy—for his clothes, money, appearance, fame?

What kind of hero does the world need?

Heroes of the Coop

Using the four values listed in the first paragraph as your tentative definition of a hero, list some actions by each of these characters that would qualify him/her to be a hero.

Chaunticleer	Mundo Cani	John Wesley Weasel	Pertelote

2. Which of Pertelote's heroic actions were taken against a visible evil?

3. Which were taken against more subtle evils or problems?

4. Are her deeds admirable? Why or why not?

5. What was her important accomplishment in the final chapter?

6. How is she different from the Pertelote in "The Nun's Priest's Tale?"

Flawed Heroes and Ordinary Mortals

Directions: Read the following in preparation for a writing assignment.

Some heroes have physical flaws. Cyrano de Bergerac, like Mundo Cani, had a big nose about which he was very sensitive.

Others have personal, spiritual, or moral flaws, which are far more important. They hinder the hero, often keep him from thinking clearly or acting wisely, yet they also show him to be human.

Ordinary mortals—and animals—also have these flaws but are basically decent people while others are basically bad but have some decent characteristics.

Let's look at some of these flaws:

Chaunticleer
> sinned as a young rooster
> was full of self-pity
> angered easily
> was proud
> hated Mundo Cani
> lost hope

Mundo Cani
> let self-pity keep him from acting
> let others take advantage of him

Pertelote
> feared to trust Chaunticleer
> yielded to fear and anger after battle

John Wesley Weasel
> used to steal eggs
> wanted revenge on Rat
> gave up hope because of his anger

Lord Russel
> fell asleep instead of watching Pins

Beryl
> left Pins to complain to Chaunticleer

And, the reverse is one who did one *good* deed:

Ebenezer Rat
> killed a Basilisk

Your turn to write:

1. Choose one of the "Good Guys" from the list of heroes. Using information from **Handouts 23** and **24** (and any additional information), characterize him/her as a hero with inevitable flaws.

2. We see Beryl as reporter of stolen eggs, nurse to Pertelote, predictor of fertility at the wedding, nursemaid to the Pins, a bearer of superstition, and an innocent victim of the Basilisks of evil. Discuss Beryl. Tell the kind of person she is, why we admire her, and why she can be considered an innocent.

3. Compare Lord Russell to his counterpart in "The Nun's Priest's Tale." Include his redeeming features in the novel and the roll of rue in the story.

4. Ebenezer Rat could be called a naturally evil "person"—his nature makes him steal eggs. Compare him to one of the purposefully evil characters in the novel.

5. A very small hero was Mouse in the land of Senex. His wife later was brave in her own way. Use these two to show that physical size and strength are not requirements for heroism.

The Coop as a Community

Directions: In your small groups, discuss and share results.

Most communities are similar in that they have the same types of stores, churches, schools, and the same types of people with the same range of values.

The Coop had no stores or schools, but it *was* a community, in both peacetime and war. Each Coop resident and each "suburban" animal who came in time of crisis is a type which can be found in your own community.

In your small group discuss the minor characters in **Handout 21**—what they were like, what they did while in or around the Coop.

Decide what type of *person* each animal suggests. There is no one and only right answer; make sure your choice corresponds with the information you find.

After you finish, compare your results to those of the other groups. Have you concluded that communities are similar? Is the author making any timeless, universal observations.

Lesson 7
Good and Evil

Objectives
- To increase awareness of the eternal battle between good and evil
- To observe that good men can repress evil qualities

Notes to the Teacher
This book is about good and evil. These lessons leave opportunities for extending discussions beyond the handouts.

Wangerin has developed believable characters. Some evil ones, like Senex and Toad, have some redeeming features; some good ones have major and minor flaws. When Chaunticleer curses God for taking his children, when Pertelote loses her courage in the dark on the battleground near the innocent dead near Nimbus, the reader may empathize and understand why they are not acting like comic-book heroes.

Medieval myths include the Toad's hatching the eggs of the Cockatrice. The Toad as enforcer is Wangerin's invention. The definition of the Antichrist is greatly simplified and may be amplified if a student would like a research task.

Procedure
1. Distribute **Handout 27**. Ask students to read the summary of the Faust legend and to answer the questions.
   Suggested Responses:
   1. *He bargains for a son and for new life for himself.*
   2. *Hope, an egg, a scaly chick with a red eye*
   3. *Senex's child kills him.*
   4. *Careless about crows; apologizes; hurts hens; selfish; yields to temptation*
   5. *The dream promising him a miraculous son; his statement "This is my son;" the son will rule over them; animals witness the birth; the seventh day it grew a tail (7th day is religious but not involved in the birth of Christ)*
   6. *In chapter 5 he is "poor Toad" who is forced to sit on the egg and does so out of fear. In chapter 11 he has become the enforcer and the spokesman for Cockatrice. He loves his power and is cruel to the animals.*
   7. *He grew afraid of Cockatrice and believed he was losing his position. He told in order to restore his power.*
   8. *Both inadvertently brought about their own deaths by setting up the situations. Both were killed by creatures they nurtured.*
   9. *Most of the evil, pagan acts of the "Antichrist" take place under the Oak.*

2. Distribute **Handout 28**. Discuss the use of Evil as a metaphor. Answer the questions.
   Suggested Responses:
   1. *They are repelled by evil.*
   2. *During his dream (Note that as Wyrm became more effective, the odor became more pervasive.)*
   3. *The bees made a paste of flower petals and sealed the floor of the Coop with it.*
   4. *rue (found by the Fox)*
   5. *It made him keep lunging, driving the spike deeper into his body.*
   6. *Evil cannot be ultimately defeated.*
   7. *He feels alone and isolated without Mundo Cani.*

3. Distribute **Handout 29**. In small groups, read the information and discuss two major questions. Share conclusions with the class.

4. Distribute **Handout 30**. Ask students to answer the questions related to the *Lord of the Coop.*
   Suggested Responses:
   1. *He loves them. At the end of chapter 19, he tells Mundo Cani, "A Rooster needs a Dog. A Rooster has come to love him. Stay."*
   2. *The Dun Cow speaks to them. He believed they were conspiring against him.*
   3. *The death of the Pins*
   4. *Intensity of emotion caused by grief, fear, etc. can evoke hatred. It is closely akin to love.*
   5. *Before, he had no one to talk to. After, his worm of worry about the river made him forget he could talk to her.*
   6. *He is above everyone else; no one can speak to him as an equal.*

7. *By lying down next to him and, in effect, absorbing and healing his worry by suffering with him*
8. *"I love you."*
9. *By sacrificing her horn*
10. *He believes the fight is unwinnable.*
11. *He detested Mundo Cani.*

5. Distribute **Handout 31**. Ask students to consider the use of the mirror image and to answer the questions.
   Suggested Responses:
   1. *Their situations are the same but their personalities and handling of the situations are totally different. Chaunticleer loves his children and his wife. Cockatrice used his "wives" to produce children he can use for evil ends.*
   2. *The word mirror is used on pages 183, 189, 192, 193, and 207. It is suggested on page 73 when Pertelote, explaining her fear of him, says, "I was afraid of what I saw in you." Cockatrice is what Chaunticleer could have become if he had not controlled his cruel tendencies and had yielded to temptation.*
   3. *He cuts off his head and carries it (like Macbeth and Macbeth's slayer). He commits a cruel act to show his pleasure in having killed.*

6. Distribute **Handout 32**. Assign the writing of a love story, retold, transposing the novel's romances into current time and people.

Senex and Toad

Directions: Read the following summary of the Faust legend, and answer the questions.

A man named Faust wanted something he could not have—wealth, power, the ability to speak to people long dead, youth and strength, success—and brooded about his inability to get what he wanted. The Devil appeared and offered Faust a deal: You get what you want for seven years and then I get your soul. Faust made the bargain and enjoyed his ill-gotten gains. When the seven years were up, he tried to cheat the Devil. The Devil won.

Over hundreds of years, many stories, novels, plays, and movies have been based on the Faust legend. The Faust character has been everything from a philosopher, a farmer, to a middle-aged man who wants to be a baseball star. The story is intriguing because human beings find it hard to resist temptation.

1. In what way is Senex a Faust character?

2. What was his reward?

3. How did the Devil get his due?

4. How does Senex differ from Chaunticleer?

5. Cockatrice could be called an Antichrist—a creature born to evil, whose birth and life parallel that of Christ in a sinister way. In chapter 5, what statements or events parallel the birth of Christ or other religious events?

6. How does Toad change between chapters 5-11? Why is he considered an evil character?

7. Why did he tell on Pertelote?

8. Why are the deaths of both Senex and Toad ironic?

9. The Terebinth Oak, in the Old Testament, is sacred to Pagans. How is its use in the novel appropriate?

The Odor of Evil

Directions: Examine the use of odor to convey the concept of *Evil*. Answer the questions.

Evil is a metaphor throughout the book. From the beginning, the reader becomes aware of its presence. Its presence is sensed through the image of odor.

Wyrm smells because of his rotting skin.

Cockatrice smells of death.

1. The animals in the land of Senex are sickened and repelled by the stench they believe comes from the body of Senex. Some die. Symbolically what do these reactions show about the animals?

2. When did Chaunticleer first notice the smell?

3. How did the animals in the Coop deal with the smell of Wyrm?

4. What smell did the animals use for protection from evil?

5. How did Cockatrice's hatred of Chaunticleer assure his death?

6. At the end Wyrm is blinded—and enraged—by Mundo Cani and the earth closes over both of them, alive in the Nether World. What does the fact that Wyrm still lives say to us?

7. After the earth closes on Mundo Cani, Chaunticleer borrows his word and says, "Marooned." What does this mean?

Name _____

Date _____

Mundo Cani Dog

Directions: In your group, discuss the questions. Share conclusions.

- Who can fail to laugh at—and love—Mundo Cani Dog as he blubbers and apologizes and gets (literally) walked on by the lowest of the animals?

- Who has not felt marooned and unloved? Who has not felt self-pity?

- But how many have suffered as Mundo Cani did silently and endured suffering?
    Chaunticleer pecks him.
    Ebenezer Rat bites his nose, which swells to double its size.
    Seven tiny Mice bite the inside of his mouth.
    Ocellata bites a path across his back.

He is swift as the wind. His eyes are "soft and full of an inexpressible sorrow." He is scoffed at by Chaunticleer and ignored by the Turkeys, but he goes on with his weeping, his acting as a table for Chaunticleer, and his rescuing of animals. He is grateful for insults and feels he deserves any harm done to him. He weeps for himself, but he also weeps for others.

He is a wimp, an underdog, a scapegoat, a whiner, a constant crier, a doormat.

And he is the one chosen—destined—for the ultimate sacrifice: to give his life for others.

Theologian Michael Berenbaum said, "The good is simple. It's not something heroic or extraordinary, it's just a simple deed done with a certain naïvetè! That's its awesome power."[1]

Discuss these questions with your group.

1. How does Wangerin foreshadow Mundo Cani's ultimate act of Good?

2. What does he seem to be saying by having a character like Dog turn out to be the sacrificial hero?

[1]*Parade Magazine*, 19 August 1990, 7.

Lord of the Coop

Directions: Read the details below and answer the questions.

Part A:

The good Chaunticleer, suffering from the murder of his three children, lectures John Wesley Weasel on hatred:

"Never again in this Coop or on this land do I want to hear that you hate a living soul."

The Weasel, like many angry people, replies, "One wants hating. Pleads for hating. Kills for hating."

Not only do Wyrm and Cockatrice hate, but, in addition to John Wesley, so do some of the good animals.
 The hens hate the Rat.
 Pertelote hates (and fears) Cockatrice.
 Beryl briefly hates the Ants.
 John Wesley hates the Basilisks for killing Wee Widow Mouse.

Ironically, the most frequent hater among the good animals is Chaunticleer who, at varying times, hates Mundo Cani, Pertelote, Cockatrice, God, and himself. At one point he savors the pain of hating.

1. What is the other emotion he feels for those listed above (excluding Cockatrice)?

2. What brings about his hatred of Pertelote and Mundo Cani?

3. What causes his hatred of God?

4. How can a basically good person hate others?

5. Chaunticleer also suffers from loneliness before and after he meets Pertelote. What are the causes of this loneliness?

6. Why is a Lord or King often lonely?

Part B:

Faith creates a problem for Chaunticleer. At the council he encourages the animals' faith. When he briefly loses his faith the night before the battle, the Dun Cow restores it. The next morning he discovers the animals' lack of faith which let the Basilisks into the camp. He helps Pertelote restore her faith the night before his battle. After his fight with Cockatrice he loses hope, faith, and "a sense of the truth." As a hero, he is doomed if he cannot reconcile his darker impulses.

7. How does the Dun Cow restore his faith the first time?

8. What does he surprise himself by saying to her?

9. How does she restore his faith the next time?

10. Why does he give up after his fight?

11. What is the cause of his misery—his sin—at the end of the book?

Mirrors

Directions: Observe the mirror image, and respond to the questions.

We have seen that a good person like Chaunticleer can have some bad qualities, some weaknesses.

Wangerin forces us to look closer at Chaunticleer by using the image of a mirror. In what way is our image in a mirror always distorted? Can we *ever* actually see ourselves as others see us? Do we really want to?

Chaunticleer's mirror image is Cockatrice.

- Cockatrice is the spiritual son of Wyrm.
- Chaunticleer, as the river continues to rise, has a "worm in his soul."

- Cockatrice has a home—the Terebinth Oak.
- Chaunticleer has a home—the Coop.

- Cockatrice takes pleasure in his children.
- Chaunticleer is proud of his children.

1. How are these things mirror images or distortions?

2. When Pertelote first sees Chaunticleer, she screams, thinking he is Cockatrice. Five times in the book Cockatrice is called Chaunticleer's mirror. Find the instances and determine what point Wangerin is making by using the mirror image (*speculum*).

3. What action does Chaunticleer take after defeating Cockatrice? In what way does this action mirror Cockatrice?

Note: Chaunticleer's difficulty in flying during his battle was caused by the loss of a primary feather from each wing. He sacrificed these in order to stop Ebenezer Rat, just as the Dun Cow sacrificed one of her horns to help Chaunticleer.

Love Stories

Directions: Follow instructions in writing your transposed story.

Every book needs a good love story and this one has more than one.

There is brotherly love—Chaunticleer loves his animals—and spiritual love—Chaunticleer loves God and the Dun Cow. Wee Widow Mouse loves her children. Mouse loved freedom, back in Senex's land.

But there is romantic love also: the comic love of two mismatched creatures, John Wesley Weasel and Wee Widow Mouse, a love which ends in tragedy, and the romantic love between Chaunticleer and his beautiful Pertelote.

Choose one of these love stories; transpose the characters into present day people. Retell the story, adding elements from the present as substitutes for those in the story. For example, Cockatrice could be a neighborhood "tough," a drug dealer or a fanatic foreign tyrant. Make sure your characters have the same traits that they do in the novel.

Lesson 8
Order and Disorder

Objectives
- To illustrate Wangerin's theme
- To point out that the war against evil is unending

Notes to the Teacher

Order and chaos is a major theme in this novel. According to Wangerin, *water*, to the Hebrews, was a factor of chaos—wild water. In the story, the river's flooding is likely a version of Noah's flood, brought about by mankind's unrighteousness. Since God apparently sent the rains which caused the river to flood, it would seem that He was punishing the animals, suggesting the question of whether they deserved punishment or whether God was unfair to them. Cockatrice takes advantage of the flood and adds the Basilisks (evil) to the river. (In his dream, Chaunticleer sees the heads.)

This lesson includes "river" quotations which even in their truncated form, not only paint a fascinating picture, but also reveal Wangerin's gift for metaphorical language. The use of this literary device affords an opportunity for extended discussion of the effects.

The dream sequences in the novel are important. Chaunticleer's dream, in which he is tempted by the river (the devil) to enact his jealousy and hatred, teaches him a lesson as well as foreshadows events. He refuses to yield to temptation. Senex, however, yields and believes what in his dreams he is told. His yielding to temptation enables Wyrm to break through God's barrier. Wyrm, "dreamed dreams below," planning to diminish earth and cancel heaven. He also yields to his temptation.

Wangerin based the first battle on facts from a book on trench warfare, *Faces of War*. Knowing that making Chaunticleer the ultimate hero would cheapen the story, he realized that the third battle had to be sacrificial, since evil cannot be overcome by brute force. War is the ultimate of disorder. Although peace came to the land after the war, the land was scorched and barren, many were dead, guilt was felt. Medieval order was restored: God was in His heaven, man was on earth, and evil was sealed inside the earth.

Procedure

1. Distribute **Handout 33** for students to chart elements of order and chaos.
   Suggested Responses:

Order	Chaos
The canonical crows	Senex giving wrong crows or unable to crow
Chaunticleer	Cockatrice
animals cooperating at work before battle	Basilisks advancing; animals in near rebellion
the Coop	river; Senex's land; Terebinth Oak
the Ants	Turkeys
the Dun Cow	Wyrm
peace	war
snow, sunshine	rain

   1. Crowed compline to calm the rebels—recited every name
   2. Against the Basilisks in the first battle

2. Distribute **Handout 34** for students to answer the questions.
   Suggested Responses:
   1. The capturing of Ebenezer Rat
   2. Squat in mud to heal wounds
   3. Wee Widow Mouse found; Pertelote found; God sent the Dun Cow.
   4. Chaunticleer hated it. ("His soul itself was damp.") The animals were happy together within the Coop.
   5. Black rain
   6. God saw that Senex's land had yielded to Wyrm, so he shut the earth in darkness and the rains began.
   7. a. The wedding
      b. Housecleaning, children tumbling, Mundo Cani grinning
      c. The holiday games, picnics, and dances
   8. It can add to the emotion of the scene or foreshadow an ironic event.
   9. Snow represents purification.

3. Distribute **Handout 35** for small group discussion of *river* quotes. Students are to read *all* of the quotations and then draw conclusions as directed.

4. Distribute **Handout 36** for small group discussion of *dreams*.
Suggested Responses:
1. Chaunticleer's dreams—*He had good dreams right after rescuing Pertelote (64), but in chapter 14 he has a dream "which goes into him." In this dream he sees his animals on the river in boats; all pass him up on his island. He tells them he hates them. When the boats return, all the animals are dead. Then he declares his hatred of the river and the island sinks.*
Significance—*He learns the searing results of hatred and realizes that he can choose against evil. The dream shows us that he is capable of hating others, as he reveals several times later, but that he can control his urges. He does choose against evil and fights it throughout the book.*
2. Senex's dream—*His dreams; make his hens seem evil and avaricous. They sympathize with him for his loss of power and tempt him with the promise of a son and of a rebirth for himself. They even speak for him, telling the hens to leave the coop. (The dreams are referred to as if they are people.) (27-29)*
Significance—*The dream feeds on his ego and his weakness. Because it promises him a son to relive his life through, he allows evil to be born— Cockatrice—and loses his life. Cockatrice will instigate the key events in the novel.*
3. Wyrm's dreams—*He dreams of destroying earth, his prison, canceling heaven, and spreading chaos. (89)*
Significance—*He had a large grudge against God and the world, which he later took out on Chaunticleer, who was guarding the earth for God. The dream reveals the kind of "person" he is and how dangerous an enemy he will be.*

5. Distribute **Handout 37** for students to complete.

Suggested Responses:

Battle	Hero(es)	Other Brave Fighters	Loser	Cost
1.	John Wesley	Ants, Mundo Cani	Basilisks	many dead
2.	Chaunticleer	-	Cockatrice	his faith
3.	Mundo Cani	-	Wyrm	Mundo Cani gone to Netherworld

4. *Wyrm is only wounded. He is still angry and will undoubtedly try again to defeat the animals.*

70

Order and Chaos

Directions: Complete the chart and answer the questions below. The Greeks created the word *chaos*: the world before order was introduced, before stars were in their places and before life was on earth. The Gods brought order to the universe. In the Bible, the book of Genesis describes a kind of chaos which ended when God closed the waters above from the waters below and gave the world order.

Later when God sent the Flood, chaos ruled again.

So, too the Coop moved from order to chaos.

Fill in the chart below with the elements of *chaos* that parallel the elements of *order.*

Order	Chaos
the canonical crows	
Chaunticleer	
animals cooperating at work before the battle	
the Coop	
the Ants	
the Dun Cow	
peace	
snow; sunshine	

1. At what point in the story did Chaunticleer use his crows to calm people during chaos?

2. At what point did he use Crows Potens?

Folklore note: An Irish folklore, a cock born in March can banish supernatural spirits by crowing.

Name _____
Date _____

Rain, Rain, Go Away

Directions: Answer the following questions.

> Rain, Rain, go away
> Come again some other day.

What if it does not go away? What if it continues every day and night, unending? Would you like Chaunticleer, realize that the rain is not merely an element of weather but something unnatural, a sign of chaos in the universe?

1. The rain started as what event was happening?

2. Because of the rain, what folk medicine was Chaunticleer able to practice?

3. What important events occurred during the rain?

4. How did the rain affect the mood of the animals?

5. What was Chaunticleer's spewing his children into the river described as?

6. What is the explanation of the origin of the rains ?

7. When events or characters' moods parallel the weather, the literary device is termed "pathetic fallacy" (a woman hysterically sobbing as she walks through a rain storm). What events parallel these weather changes?

   a. snow

   b. spring

   c. end of rain in chapter 15

8. Why would an author use "pathetic fallacy?" How does it affect these scenes?

9. Rain traditionally symbolizes purification since it comes from Heaven. Since God sent the clouds that covered the land, He apparently sent the rain also. Do you believe it symbolizes purification here? Why or why not? What other weather event might suggest purification?

The River

Directions: With your group read these descriptions of the river. Discuss the changes, actions, and symbolism of the river. How does the river contribute to the chaos of the world? (Page numbers are included for reference to text. See Teacher Notes on page vii for edition used.)

1. "Why should the river move fast?" (49)

2. ". . . so much water and so great a current, choked with so many logs, branches, and shunt, made not a sound at all." (55)

3. "(Cockatrice dropped) a black rain of Basilisks into the river." (85)

4. "The river began to boil." (87)

5. "It was the river that was confusing and troubling [Chaunticleer]." (96)

6. "The good river had become a destruction, silently swallowing Chaunticleer's land foot by foot. It scoured the earth away from the roots of the trees . . . until they collapsed . . . it swallowed near-by hills . . . "(97)

7. "The water stank with such a loathsome odor that the Rooster could not breathe without gagging." (99)

8. "It is the river that has worried me for so long. It's flooded the entire south territory of my land— a strange, unholy flood." (105)

9. "A sea! The waters looked like an endless sea covering half the earth and reaching toward this place. The sea was all afire . . . It burned with an ungodly color." (148)

10. ". . . he saw that the waters of the river were seething. Where the demon's head had entered them, the waters were boiling." (209)

11. "The river is at the wall of the camp." (215)

12. "Mountainous, furious waves, foaming in their rage, slammed into the wall, leaped straight toward the sky, hissed and sprayed everywhere, then rained back down as from a storm." (221)

13. "A mysterious confusion struck the waves of the sea: Instead of their rhythmic rolling toward the camp, there was a dizzy turning. They slapped and struggled against one another, giants without direction. They came together, these waves, like enormous hands, clapping." (224)

14. "The chasm was drinking the entire sea before it, and the sea rushed into it like suicide." (224)

15. "And the water, when finally it hit Wyrm's flesh, steamed." (225)

16. "The sea above simply stumbled, as if surprised in its forward walk by a dropoff: The sea stumbled, then settled much lower than it was before." (228)

17. "And finally, between him and the sea, an endless scar. . . . " (228)

Dreams

Directions: With your group members, discuss the dream sequences and their significance of Chaunticleer, Senex, and Wyrm.

In the 1920s, Sigmund Freud published his book on the psychology of dreams, a subject everyone believed to be new. But people were dreaming and interpreting dreams eons before Freud:

- dreams interpreted by Joseph in the Old Testament
- dreams that Pertelote interpreted
- dreams that Chaucer's Calpurnia and Decius Brutus interpreted for Julius Caesar

Some believe that dreams reveal dangers, disorders, secrets, truths. The dream world is included in the works of many novelists, playwrights, musical-comedy writers, and script writers.

The Dreamer

In this novel, Beryl is a character who manipulates dreams. She offers to give Pertelote a potion to douse her dreams, but it is her superstitions that serve as warnings.

Three other characters have significant dreams: Chaunticleer, Senex, and Wyrm.

For each, find the dream sequences in the text. Determine the significance of each dream. What does it reveal about the character or his future?

Notice that Wangerin uses smell (the odor of evil) as a crossover from Chaunticleer's dream to reality.

Name _____

Date _____

War and Peace

Directions: Complete the chart below and the ensuing questions.

The greatest cause of disorder in any land is war. Laws and moral codes are broken ("Thou shalt not kill"), populations annihilated, buildings destroyed. Nature is critically wounded; chaos often reigns.

Chaunticleer has no choice: to cure the disorder in his land he must participate in a greater disorder: war. His war is not against another country. It is a war against Evil, the ultimate enemy.

1. Fill in the chart of the three battles of Chaunticleer's war:

Battle	Hero(es)	Other Brave Fighters	Loser	Cost
1.				
2.				
3.				

2. Was the cost too great in any of the battles? Why or why not?

3. A Pyrrhic victory is one in which the winner pays such a great price for the victory that it is meaningless. Were any of Chaunticleer's victories Pyrrhic?

4. At the end of the story, the seam of the earth closes on the blinded Wyrm and he is again imprisoned, but the land, lies in ruin. Why is this not a happy ending for the book (aside from Mundo Cani's loss)? What does Wangerin want readers to realize?

Lesson 9
Beyond Earthly Knowledge

Objectives
- To become aware of religious allusions and overtones
- To become aware of allegorical elements

Notes to the Teacher
Although this book is not classified under *religion* by the Dewey decimal system, it, never the less, does contain a number of both obvious and subtle religious allusions and overtones which need to be perceived in order to grasp the full meaning of the novel.

God is not a character but a catalyst, a provoker, a stage director. He turns Chaunticleer from cynicism and cruelty and makes him a keeper; he imprisons Wyrm; he sends clouds and rain; he sends the Dun Cow. God is not part of the Good trinity, Chaunticleer wears many biblical hats: Saul/Paul, Moses, Job, David, Noah, and perhaps, within the Coop, God. Since Wangerin did not purpose to write an allegory, characters will not fit neatly into only one slot, leaving the way open for logical arguments for placing the same characters in different positions in the trinities and allegory.

Included in this lesson is an allegory assignment, and in the Supplementary Materials is a student sample of a World War II analogy.

Procedure
1. Distribute **Handout 38**. Discuss the sources and use of mystical numbers. Ask students to give additional examples.
   Suggested Responses:

   2.

3	7
weapons	mice
types of crows	canonical crows
enemies	days before tail grew on Cockatrice
battles	
pins	words from Wyrm
fights with Cockatrice	7th crow to calm animals

   3. Some deal with a sense of order.
   4. Wyrm, Cockatrice, Basilisks
      (Cockatrice can be considered an anti-Christ figure.)
   5. Chaunticleer, Mundo Cani, Dun Cow
      (Wangerin thought of the Dun Cow as a symbol of the Holy Ghost as he wrote the book. He later realized that Mundo Cani was a Christ figure. However, students can give different answers as long as they can defend the answers).
   6. They give a sense of order, of balance, and a feeling that super-natural powers are at work.

2. Distribute **Handout 39**. Discuss the meaning of *allusion*. Ask students to give examples by writing phrases or sentences containing an allusion. Complete the assignment on the handout.
   Suggested Responses:
   1. a conniving woman
   2. a strong man
   3. a cruel, despotic person
   4. a shy dreamer
   5. either an angelic woman or a way-out, shocking person
   6. Job
   7. David (at Absalom's death)
   8. Saul/Paul

3. Distribute **Handout 40**. Discuss the meaning of *allegory*. Ask students to give examples familiar to them before answering the questions and doing the writing assignment.
   Suggested Responses:
   1. It teaches a lesson in a simple way. The Coop is reminiscent of American society.
   2. It is allegorical style: animals as characters; epic style (hero, major battles, etc.); touches of satire.
   3. (Example: Nimbus—innocence)
   4. Chaunticleer—by the river (using jealousy); Wyrm—by power; Senex—by promise of a child, renewed youth and power
   5. She is the comforter, the compassionate one; reveals what sharing suffering can do to heal the sufferer.

Mystical Numbers

Directions: Read the details and complete the handout.

Throughout history, certain numbers have had mystical associations. Though not always consistent in signification, they frequently had some association with religion—Christian, Jewish, Islamic, etc. Sometimes there is no symbolic meaning, merely the suggestion of something otherworldly, beyond man's comprehension.

You will find mystical numbers used in many subjects; religion, superstition, mythology, literature. You are probably best acquainted with mystical numbers as used in fairy tales.

1. Test your fairy-tale IQ. Name some fairy tale or nursery rhyme examples of the most common mystical numbers: 3, 7, and 12.

    Example: Three blind mice

    The numbers even extend into our calendar: the 7-day week, the 12-month year. In superstition, the third time is the charm; seven years of bad luck for breaking a mirror.

2. Two numbers are used frequently in *The Book of the Dun Cow*: 3 and 7. Find as many examples of each as you can:

    3   **7**

3. What might the 3s and 7s represent? (Note the context of the occurrences.)

4. Another religious use of three is the Trinity: a group of three individuals or entities who are part of a single whole. Wangerin has set up two trinities in his book: a Good Trinity and an Evil Trinity. The Evil Trinity is easy to determine. Who make up the Trinity? Place them in order of power, with the most powerful one at the top.

5. The Good Trinity may be a little trickier to determine. Think in Christian terms: Father, Son, and Holy Ghost. Do not use God in your Trinity. Set up your version of the Good Trinity in the same top to bottom order. Be prepared to defend your choices.

6. What does the use of Trinities add to the novel?

Name _____

Date _____

Allusions

Directions: Answer the following questions on the topic of allusions.

An *allusion* is an indirect reference to the nature or qualities of a known person, place, or thing. If a woman is called a Venus, the reader knows she is like the beautiful Greek goddess. You would readily understand what was meant if someone said, "Bill moves like Michael Jackson." If a person meets his Waterloo, our knowledge of Napoleon tells us that the person has been defeated.

What would these allusions mean? Add several familiar to you from literature, history, foreign language, or daily conversation.

1. a Jezebel

2. a Samson

3. a Hitler

4. a Walter Mitty

5. a Madonna

In *The Book of the Dun Cow*, what biblical characters are alluded to in these passages?

6. Chaunticleer: "You, God, promise—then break promises. You give. You warm me to your gift. You cause love to go out of me to your gift—and then you kill me. You kill my gift."

7. Chaunticleer: "My sons, my sons. Why didn't God let me die instead of you?"

8. (The young Chaunticleer kills the Wolf and plans to kill the leaders of the land.) "But during the night, while the Rooster waited in a tree, the Lord appeared to him. The light was so bright that the Rooster fell out of his tree, stunned, full of terror." After speaking to him, the Lord tells him to go to the Northern land. "So mighty, so glorious was the force of that final command that the Rooster both died and got up at once."

Allegory

Directions: Read the following allegory. Apply the term to the novel.

> As Joe Allofus walked down the road, he met Harry Greed, who was wearing several solid gold chains and a Rolex watch and was polishing his Porsche.
>
> "Hey, Joe," said Greed. "How do you like this red baby?"
>
> "It's rad!" said Allofus, noting the expensive stereo system blaring inside and the gold hubcaps.
>
> "How would you like to own one? Be better than all the rest of the guys?" asked Greed.
>
> Joe Allofus was tempted. What a chance this was! Then he looked at Greed's face, noting the swollen cheeks, the shifty eyes, and the sneer on his mouth. Did he want to be like Harry Greed? He said, "I'm sorry but I'm in a rush," and hurried down the road where his fiancée, Faith, was waiting.

This anecdote is an example of an allegory. Wherein characters often have names suggesting their traits and actions in correspondence with their qualities. *Everyman*, a famous allegory from the medieval period is a play about man's temptations. In the seventeenth century, John Bunyan wrote *Pilgrim's Progress*, a masterpiece of religious allegory.

However, some attempts at pure allegory result in flat, stilted characters. As a consequence, many writers prefer to include allegorical elements without assigning one character as a representative of a single quality. This choice of approach allows writers to create attention-getting plots with credible characters.

This is the choice Walter Wangerin made. He wrote what he calls a *parable* but what he is pleased to have others call a *beast fable*.

1. In what ways is the book a parable?

2. In what sense is it a beast fable?

3. If we were to oversimplify the book and consider it an allegory, state what *major* characteristic or quality each character would represent.

Chaunticleer

Pertelote

John Wesley Weasel

Mundo Cani

Cockatrice

The Dun Cow

Wyrm

Basilisks

Lord Russel

The Pins

Beryl

Ebenezer Rat

The Ants

The Turkeys

Nimbus

4. Allegories often deal with temptation. What characters in this book were tempted? Who or what tempted them?

5. Think about the Dun Cow; when she appears; to whom she appears; what she does or does not say; how she affects people. What is her function in the novel?

6. Optional Activity. Create a different kind of allegory using the characters in the book. Show the book as an allegory of World War II, the Cold War, the War on Poverty, or your choice of any event or topic which you think will fit the category.

Lesson 10
Imagery and Beyond

Objectives
- To observe the beauty of Wangerin's use of language
- To compare *Animal Farm* and *The Book of the Dun Cow*

Notes to the Teacher

Wangerin's novel is distinguished by the beauty of its language. This lesson is designed to focus student attention on the author's art in creating effective imagery and to develop skills in using literary devices to convey images.

Students are also directed to a comparison of the two novels in this lesson. If your students did not read *Animal Farm*, omit **Handout 43**.

Procedure

1. Distribute **Handout 41**. Ask students to label the types of imagery in the quotes and to explain their effectiveness.
   Suggested Responses:

1.	S	10. S
2.	M, P	11. S
3.	M	12. M
4.	M	13. M
5.	P	14. M, P
6.	S	15. M, P
7.	S	*(The numbers 1 and 12*
8.	M	*are humorous.)*
9.	S	

2. Distribute **Handout 42** for students to write *found poems*. Suggest passages on following pages to assist students who may find it difficult to locate appropriate lines: 22, 63, 70, 89, 135-138, 147, 202, 210.

3. Distribute **Handout 43** for students in small groups to use as a review in comparing *Animal Farm* and *The Book of the Dun Cow*.

4. Distribute **Handout 44** for students to select a topic for writing a theme. The assignment may be used as an optional activity or for evaluation.

Poetry in Prose I

Directions: In a prose work, a good author often writes poetic imagery.

Label the following quotations from the novel as simile, metaphor, or personification. Be able to explain why they are effective. Point out which are humorous images.

_____ 1. "[Chaunticleer] set to pecking the great nose in front of him as if it were a piano."

_____ 2. "When Chaunticleer crowed his canonical crows, the day wore the right kind of clothes."

_____ 3. "His soul itself was damp."

_____ 4. "[The river was] a spinning cemetery of bones."

_____ 5. "The naked trees shivered."

_____ 6. "She hummed for him a quiet melody like ringing crystal."

_____ 7. "The rain drove at the earth as if it were intent on digging craters."

_____ 8. "[Pertelote's] silence was a suffocation for him and her distance a torment."

_____ 9. "Like flowing sand [the Ants] closed upon the Coop."

_____ 10. "[The Dog] came like the wind, streaking ninety degrees around 10,000 animals."

_____ 11. "[The word *Wyrm*] came like disease and hung foul in the air."

_____ 12. "To Mundo Cani: "Why, you're a pump! You're a running pump! Who flushes you every time I look around?"

_____ 13. "The sky was a stone—hollowed underneath, hard, pure white, hot, a lid locked over the whole earth."

_____ 14. "He made a whip out of his crowing, and he lashed the serpents with it."

_____ 15. "The sea above simply stumbled, as if surprised in its forward walk by a drop-off."

Poetry in Prose II

Directions: Read the poem and instructions for writing a *found poem*.

Pertelote: A Love Song

He saw her lying open,
Where anyone in the world
Could have come by
And hurt her.

He saw her loose,
Sleeping,
And without protection whatsoever.

He saw her truthful,
When she was not pretending
To be anything else than
A purely white Hen
With fire at her throat.

He saw her
When she didn't see him back.

He saw her
Lovely.

Do you consider this a poem? It is in verses and stanzas; it has imagery, repetition, rhythm, sound devices. It looks and sounds like a poem.

Actually, it is six lines of a prose paragraph in chapter 8. Often prose, especially in this novel, *The Book of the Dun Cow*, reads like poetry. Poetry created by extracting sentences from a section of prose and breaking them into lines is called *found poetry*.

Writing Found Poetry

Look for a description that flows rhythmically, has poetic devices, can stand alone when removed from the prose passage. Take sentences from only one paragraph or continuous section in the original.

You may omit clauses or phrases that "show action" or contain dialogue if they interrupt the flow of the passage. Be sure to retain the meaning and grammar of the sentences.

In deciding line length, rely on your ear for rhythmic flow and on your knowledge of grammar. A line usually ends on a strong word: noun; verb; adjective. It is often composed of a grammatical unit: clause; prepositional phrase; verb phrase.

Use one-word lines rarely, if at all. The example, "Pertelote: A Love Song", uses two of them: the first,

"Sleeping," is set off in the prose passage with commas, which suggests that it can stand alone. Had it been attached to the line above or below, the rhythm would have been disrupted. The final word and line, "Lovely," is set apart for emphasis since it summarizes what Chaunticleer felt for Pertelote.

Become a found poet, using *The Book of the Dun Cow* as your source.

Name _____
Date _____

Sly Pigs and Cocky Roosters

Directions: You have now read two very different versions of the beast fable. With members of your group, summarize and review the novels by making a comparison, using the following list as a guide. You may also consider elements not on the list, if you wish. Make notes to share with the class in a general overview.

a. tone

b. style of writing

c. hero/main character

d. other characters

e. setting

f. enemies/wars

g. intended audience

h. purpose

i. moral/theme

j. ending

k. closeness to definition of "beast fable"

Essay Topics

1. Discuss Chaunticleer as a mirror of Cockatrice.

2. Compare Pertelote and Beryl.

3. Is Beryl a sympathetic character? Why or why not?

4. Compare one or two elements in the two novels. Be specific.

5. Write a newspaper story describing the three battles in news-story form or discussing environmental problems in the Land of Chaunticleer.

6. Prove this statement: The book shows that women, like men, can be brave, clever, and sensible.

7. The book opens with Mundo Cani Dog crying "Marooned!" and ends (except for the "Final Word") with Chaunticleer saying "Marooned." Discuss the significance of this word thematically in the novel. In what sense are the animals in the Coop marooned?

8. Several characters in the book make sacrifices. Discuss sacrifice as a theme using at least two or three characters as examples.

9. Discuss the novel as a parable of good and evil.

10. Prove that Chaunticleer was a good leader.

11. Compare Mundo Cani to Cyrano de Bergerac or to Lancelot in *The Once and Future King*. Include their feelings about themselves as well as their talents.

12. Compare the loyalty of the animals to Chaunticleer with that of the animals to Napoleon in *Animal Farm*.

13. Chaunticleer has many problems: self-pity, jealousy, an inability to show his compassion, loneliness, loss of faith. Show how these problems and the ways they are resolved show the humanity of Chaunticleer.

14. Chaunticleer later gets his chance to go, perhaps with John Wesley Weasel, to the Netherworld. There he encounters Mundo Cani again. In story or play form, describe their meeting. Include dialogue.

15. Discuss the role of the Dun Cow in the novel.

16. Reread the descriptions of Nimbus the Deer (who is not named until his death) and the scene in which Pertelote encounters his dead body. Explain why he is used and what point his life and death make about war.

17. Wangerin uses naturally evil characters (such as Ebenezer Rat) and purposefully evil characters (such as Cockatrice). Discuss the two types of evil, and determine what Wangerin is showing through them.

18. Prove that John Wesley Weasel is primarily a comic character.

19. The animals are isolated in their Coop just as the boys in *Lord of the Flies* are on their island. Compare their reactions to their isolation and their behavior.

20. Compare *The Book of the Dun Cow* to *The Hobbit* or *Lord of the Rings*.

21. Beryl worries about the words chanted by the Ants who are playing with the Pins; Chaunticleer is haunted by Wyrm's seven words. Discuss the importance and significance of words in the novel.

22. In what ways are the Turkeys like many people?

23. Compare the governments in *Animal Farm* and *The Book of the Dun Cow* and their effectiveness. Include the leaders' concern for their people.

24. Compare the two books as beast fables, animal tales, parables, etc.

25. Discuss temptation as a theme in the novel.

26. Defend your choice of animals for the Good Trinity.

27. Write epitaphs for Mundo Cani, Nimbus, Ebenezer, Mouse, and Wee Widow Mouse.

28. Discuss the role of Lord Russel, The Fox of Good Sense.

29. Discuss the role of the Serpent as a figure of evil in literature, mythology, and/or religion. Include Wyrm.

30. Characterize Wyrm based on his description, his words, his threats, and his temptations.

31. Prove that Mundo Cani was the right person for the final battle.

32. Write the omitted scene in which the Pins and Beryl die. Be consistent with the novel.

33. Discuss the Dun Cow as a comforter.

34. Compare Cockatrice and Chaunticleer as parents.

35. Compare Napoleon and Chaunticleer as leaders.

36. Discuss the role of weather in the novel.

37. Discuss the use and effect of the numbers 3 and 7 in the novel.

38. What is the importance of crows in the book?

39. In what sense are we, like the animals, the keepers of the earth?

40. Explain Chaunticleer's love/hate relationship with Mundo Cani Dog.

41. Write your own beast fable. Be sure it includes a lesson.

42. Write a short-short science-fiction story that uses the order/disorder theme.

Reading Aids

A: *Animal Farm* terms

knacker—butcher

trotter—foot of a pig, used for food

dissentients—those who disagree with a policy

lithograph—an engraved picture

parasitical—clinging to and getting sustenance from something else

paddock—a fenced area for horses

indefatigable—untiring

skirmishing—having a minor fight

factious—opposing groups

procured—got; received

solicitor—lawyer

chaff—leftovers from hulled grain

mangels—beets used in cattle feed

categorically—absolutely, certainly

expulsion—act of throwing someone out

retribution—act of getting even

sentinel—guard

lamentations—expressions of grief

superannuated—very old

deputation—a representative group sent somewhere

swill—pig food

Name _____
Date _____

Directions: As you come upon a new character in your reading, identify and give characteristics.

B: Characters in *Animal Farm*

Mr. Jones:

Old Major:

Napoleon:

Snowball:

Moses, the raven:

Human Beings:

Mollie:

Benjamin:

The Cat:

the sheep:

Mr. Pilkington:

Frederick:

the pigeons:

the dogs:

Squealer:

Minimus:

Mr. Whymper:

Pinkeye:

Boxer:

Clover:

Name _____
Date _____

Character Quiz

Matching. No repeats. Give letter only.

——— 1. Snowball

——— 2. Napoleon

——— 3. Boxer

——— 4. Benjamin

——— 5. Major

——— 6. Mollie

——— 7. sheep

——— 8. dogs

——— 9. Whymper

——— 10. Moses

a. hardworking common man

b. enforcers, police

c. self-centered person; lover of luxury

d. con man; propagandist

e. cruel, uncaring dictator

f. go-between

g. blind followers

h. philosopher who gives ideas

i. mother figure; one who cares for others

j. concerned; hardworking planner and leader

k. spy; gossip

l. skeptic; doubter; pessimist

Answer Key for *Animal Farm* Quiz

1. j

2. e

3. a

4. l

5. h

6. c

7. g

8. b

9. f

10. k

Name _____

Date _____

Essay Questions *(Animal Farm)*

Answer the following questions. Support your responses with references to the book.

1. What was the incident which triggered the animals' rebellion?

2. Who led the animals in the Battle of Cowshed? What courageous act did he perform? Which other animals were also heroic?

3. What happened to Snowball after he convinced the animals that they should build a windmill?

4. Who worked the hardest to build the windmills? What was his final reward?

5. List four ways the pigs changed during the course of the story.

6. Briefly summarize the chief character traits of each of the following animals in *Animal Farm*: Napoleon, Snowball, Mollie, Benjamin, Squealer, Boxer, Clover.

7. Why was Boxer's death particularly pathetic?

8. Old Major's warning on pp. 21-22 proved to be an ironic warning (prophecy). How?

9. How do Napoleon and Squealer twist and distort both logic and history to serve their own ends? What do you think of leaders who practice such deception?

10. Why do you think George Orwell used animals as the major characters in his story? How did using animals add or detract from the presentation of his theme?

11. Choose two recent historical characters and relate them to characters in *Animal Farm*. Justify your choices.

Selected Sources for Animal Tales

Key

A=   Arab
Ae=   Aesop
An=   Anansi
B=   Black
Br=   Brer Rabbit
I=   Indian
M=   Mexican

1. Abrahams, Roger D. *Afro-American Folktales*. New York: Pantheon, 1985. (An, B, Br)

2. Appiah, Peggy. *Ananse, the Spider: Tales from an Ashanti Village*. New York: Pantheon, 1966. (An)

3. Astrow, Margot, ed. *American Indian Prose and Poetry*. New York: Capricorn Books, 1962. (I)

4. Botkin, B.A., ed. *A Treasury of American Folklore*. New York: Crown, 1944. (Br, B)

5. —————— *A Treasury of Southern Folklore*. New York: Crown, 1958. (Br, B)

6. Bushnag, Inea. *Arab Folktales*. New York: Pantheon, 1986. (A)

7. Caduto, Michael and Joseph Bruchac. *Keepers of the Earth*. Golden, Colo.: Fulcrum, 1988. (I)

8. Courlander, Harold. *A Treasury of Afro-American Folklore*. New York: Crown, 1976. (An, Br, B, Haiti)

9. Dobie, J. Frank, Mody Boatright, and Harry Ransom, eds. *Coyote Wisdom*. Austin: Texas Folklore Society, 1938 (I, M)

10. Dorson, Richard M., ed. *American Negro Folktales*. Greenwich: Fawcett Publ., Inc., 1967. (B)

11. Erdoes, Richard and Alfonso Ortiz, eds. *American Indian Myths and Legends*. New York: Pantheon, 1984. (I)

12. Hughes, Langston and Arna Bontemps, eds. *The Book of Negro Folklore*. New York: Dodd, Mead, & Co., 1958. (Br)

13. Marriott, Alice and Carol K. Rachlin. *American Indian Mythology*. New York: New American Library, 1968. (I)

14. Rees, Ennis. *Fables from Aesop*. New York: Oxford University Press, 1966. (Ae)

15. Rugoff, Milton, ed. *A Harvest of World Folk Tales*. New York: Viking, 1955. (Ae, An, Br, I)

Pogo Titles

1. Kelly, Walt. *The Pogo Papers*. New York: Ultramarine Publishing, 1977.

2. Kelly, Walt. *Pogo: We Have Met the Enemy and He Is Us*. St. Louis: Fireside, 1972.

3. Kelly, Walt and Bill Crouch, Jr. *Outrageously Pogo*. St. Louis: Fireside, 1985.

Name _____
Date _____

Minor Characters Quiz
The Book of the Dun Cow

A. Matching. No repeats. Place letter to the left of the number.

_____ 1. Perfected the pout

_____ 2. Enforced the law

_____ 3. Spread the word

_____ 4. Plotted rebellion

_____ 5. Challenged Cockatrice

_____ 6. Was a storyteller

_____ 7. Stole eggs

_____ 8. Made a bargain with Evil

_____ 9. Revenged his love's death

_____ 10. Played once a year

_____ 11. Died an innocent

_____ 12. Had one eye

_____ 13. Tied children to a branch

_____ 14. Disobeyed nurse

_____ 15. Was superstitious

a. John Wesley Weasel

b. Lord Russel

c. Ebenezer Rat

d. Wee Widow Mouse

e. Pins

f. Toad

g. Tick Tock

h. Scrape

i. Senex

j. Scarce

k. Nimbus

l. Ants

m. Ocellata

n. Basilisks

o. Wyrm

p. Cockatrice

r. Beryl

s. Mouse

t. Bees

u. Turkeys

B. Matching. Which animals did these things before or during the battle? Use above list. No repeats.

_____ 16. built ramparts

_____ 17. sealed odor in the ground

_____ 18. raced up the wall

_____ 19. gathered rue

_____ 20. made Pertelote cry after the first battle

Reading Test

1. Who cried "Marooned!"

2. Who laid the egg that became Cockatrice?

3. Who was Cockatrice's enforcer?

4. Who told stories to the Pins and taught them tricks?

5. Who bit a serpent before dying?

6. How do the animals at the Council manage to learn the story of Cockatrice without yielding to panic?

7. Who saved the Turkeys from the Basilisks?

8. Of what did Ocelatta Turkey make an art?

9. What question does Chaunticleer unthinkingly ask the Dun Cow?

10. What animals climbed on top of the wall first?

11. What plant gave them protection?

12. How did Wee Widow Mouse die?

13. Who saved John Wesley?

14. Identify Gaff and Slasher.

15. After his victory, what did Chaunticleer raise high?

16. What did the Dog do when Chaunticleer turned against them and tried to die?

17. What weapon did Dog use?

18. Who hid in a hole?

19. What did Pertelote tell Chaunticleer about the Dog?

20. What was Chaunticleer's secret (or sin) concerning the Dog?

Answer Keys

Answer Key to Minor Characters quiz

1. m	11. k
2. f	12. o
3. j	13. d
4. h	14. e
5. s	15. r
6. b	16. l
7. c	17. t
8. i	18. u
9. a	19. b
10. l	20. k

Answer Key to Reading Test

1. Mundo Cani Dog

2. Senex

3. Toad

4. Lord Russel (Fox)

5. Ebenezer Rat

6. Pertelote sings it.

7. Mundo Cani

8. pouting

9. Why do I love you?

10. Turkeys

11. rue

12. bitten by hidden Basilisk

13. Mundo Cani

14. Chaunticleer's spikes

15. head of Cockatrice

16. picked him up and carried him

17. horn of the Dun Cow

18. John Wesley Weasel

19. (one of three)

He is alive.

It was his destiny to fight Wyrm.

He told her about the Dun Cow.

20. He despised him.

Name _____

Date _____

Allegorical Outline of World War II

Chaunticleer: Portrayed Stalin at the beginning but later became benevolent and became Franklin Roosevelt

Pertelote: Represented France who was originally defeated but stayed alive and hurt Germany in the end

Cockatrice: Germany's hierarchy (Himmler, Goebbels, Goering) and the military

Wyrm: Hitler

Lord Russel: Offered help and good advice to defeat the enemy; England

Tick Tock: Leader of smaller countries of Free Europe who didn't make the difference, but who were a nuisance to Hitler. The Ants made up the armies.

Nimbus: Innocence—neutral countries who were engulfed anyway

Ebenezer Rat: Italy; was a threat at the beginning but was later consumed by the greater evil

The Pins: Small, indifferent nations who felt Hitler's wrath

Mundo Cani Dog: Countries who made the most sacrifices and lost the most lives

Wee Widow Mouse: Same as the Pins except she was concerned

John Wesley Weasel: Allied soldier; Fierce fighter

Brandon West
Senior

Acknowledgments

For permission to reprint all works in this volume, grateful acknowledgment is made to the following holders of copyright, publishers, or representatives.

Whole Book
Excerpts from *Animal Farm* by George Orwell, 1946. Published by Signet Books, New American Library, New York, New York.

Whole Book
Excerpts from *The Book of the Dun Cow* by Walter Wangerin, Jr. Copyright © 1978 by Walter M. Wangerin, Jr. Reprinted by permission of HarperCollins Publishers.

Lesson 1, Handout 3
Excerpts from *Benet's Reader's Encyclopedia,* 3rd ed. by William R. Benet. Copyright (c) 1987 by William R. Benet. Reprinted by permission of HarperCollins Publishers.

Lesson 6, Handout 23
Drawing from *The Bestiary: A Book of Beasts* by T. H. White, 1960. Reprinted with permission of J. P. Putnam's Sons, New York, New York.

Novel/Drama Series

Novel

Across Five Aprils, Hunt

The Adventures of Huckleberry Finn, Twain

The Adventures of Tom Sawyer, Twain

Alice's Adventures in Wonderland/ Through the Looking-Glass, Carroll

All Creatures Great and Small, Herriot

All Quiet on the Western Front, Remarque

All the King's Men, Warren

Animal Farm, Orwell/ The Book of the Dun Cow, Wangerin, Jr.

Anna Karenina, Tolstoy

Anne Frank: The Diary of a Young Girl, Frank

Anne of Green Gables, Montgomery

The Assistant/The Fixer, Malamud

The Autobiography of Miss Jane Pittman, Gaines

The Awakening, Chopin/ Madame Bovary, Flaubert

Babbitt, Lewis

The Bean Trees/Pigs in Heaven, Kingsolver

Beowulf/Grendel, Gardner

Billy Budd/Moby Dick, Melville

Bless Me, Ultima, Anaya

Brave New World, Huxley

The Bridge of San Luis Rey, Wilder

The Brothers Karamazov, Dostoevsky

The Call of the Wild/White Fang, London

The Canterbury Tales, Chaucer

The Catcher in the Rye, Salinger

The Cay/Timothy of the Cay, Taylor

Charlotte's Web, White/ The Secret Garden, Burnett

The Chosen, Potok

The Christmas Box, Evans/ A Christmas Carol, Dickens

Chronicles of Narnia, Lewis

Cold Sassy Tree, Burns

The Count of Monte Cristo, Dumas

Crime and Punishment, Dostoevsky

Cry, the Beloved Country, Paton

Dandelion Wine, Bradbury

Darkness at Noon, Koestler

David Copperfield, Dickens

A Day No Pigs Would Die, Peck

December Stillness, Hahn/ Izzy, Willy-Nilly, Voigt

The Divine Comedy, Dante

The Dollmaker, Arnow

Don Quixote, Cervantes

Dr. Zhivago, Pasternak

Dubliners, Joyce

East of Eden, Steinbeck

Fahrenheit 451, Bradbury

A Farewell to Arms, Hemingway

Farewell to Manzanar, Houston & Houston/Black Like Me, Griffin

Frankenstein, Shelley

A Gathering of Flowers, Thomas, ed.

The Giver, Lowry

The Good Earth, Buck

The Grapes of Wrath, Steinbeck

Great Expectations, Dickens

The Great Gatsby, Fitzgerald

Gulliver's Travels, Swift

Hard Times, Dickens

Hatchet, Paulsen/Robinson Crusoe, Defoe

The Heart Is a Lonely Hunter, McCullers

Heart of Darkness, Conrad

Hiroshima,Hersey/On the Beach,Shute

The Hobbit, Tolkien

Homecoming/Dicey's Song, Voigt

The Hound of the Baskervilles, Doyle

The Human Comedy/ My Name Is Aram, Saroyan

Incident at Hawk's Hill, Eckert/ Where the Red Fern Grows, Rawls

Jane Eyre, Brontë

Johnny Tremain, Forbes

Journey of the Sparrows,Buss/Cubias/ The Honorable Prison, de Jenkins

The Joy Luck Club, Tan

Jubal Sackett/The Walking Drum, L'Amour

Julie of the Wolves, George/Island of the Blue Dolphins, O'Dell

The Jungle, Sinclair

The Killer Angels, Shaara

Le Morte D'Arthur, Malory

The Learning Tree, Parks

Les Miserables, Hugo

The Light in the Forest/ A Country of Strangers, Richter

Little House in the Big Woods/ Little House on the Prairie, Wilder

Lord of the Flies, Golding

The Lord of the Rings, Tolkien

The Martian Chronicles, Bradbury

Missing May, Rylant/The Summer of the Swans, Byars

Mrs. Mike, Freedman/I Heard the Owl Call My Name, Craven

Murder on the Orient Express/ And Then There Were None, Christie

My Antonia, Cather

The Natural, Malamud/Shoeless Joe, Kinsella

Nectar in a Sieve, Markandaya/ The Woman Warrior, Kingston

Night, Wiesel

A Night to Remember, Lord/Streams to the River, River to the Sea, O'Dell

1984, Orwell

Number the Stars, Lowry/Friedrich, Richter

Obasan, Kogawa

The Odyssey, Homer

The Old Man and the Sea,Hemingway/Ethan Frome, Wharton

The Once and Future King, White

Ordinary People, Guest/ The Tin Can Tree, Tyler

The Outsiders, Hinton/ Durango Street, Bonham

The Pearl/Of Mice and Men, Steinbeck

The Picture of Dorian Gray, Wilde/ Dr. Jekyll and Mr. Hyde, Stevenson

The Pigman/The Pigman's Legacy, Zindel

A Portrait of the Artist as a Young Man, Joyce

The Power and the Glory, Greene

A Prayer for Owen Meany, Irving

Pride and Prejudice, Austen

The Prince, Machiavelli/Utopia, More

The Prince and the Pauper, Twain

Profiles in Courage, Kennedy

Rebecca, du Maurier

The Red Badge of Courage, Crane

The Return of the Native, Hardy

Roll of Thunder, Hear My Cry/ Let the Circle Be Unbroken, Taylor

Sarum, Rutherfurd

The Scarlet Letter, Hawthorne

A Separate Peace, Knowles

Shane, Schaefer/The Ox-Bow
    Incident, Van Tilburg Clark

Siddhartha, Hesse

The Sign of the Chrysanthemum/
    The Master Puppeteer, Paterson

The Signet Classic Book of Southern
    Short Stories, Abbott and
    Koppelman, eds.

The Slave Dancer, Fox/
    I, Juan de Pareja, De Treviño

Song of Solomon, Morrison

The Sound and the Fury, Faulkner

Spoon River Anthology, Masters

The Stranger/The Plague, Camus

Summer of My German Soldier, Greene/
    Waiting for the Rain, Gordon

A Tale of Two Cities, Dickens

Talking God/A Thief of Time, Hillerman

Tess of the D'Urbervilles, Hardy

Their Eyes Were Watching God,
    Hurston

Things Fall Apart/No Longer at Ease,
    Achebe

To Kill a Mockingbird, Lee

To the Lighthouse, Woolf

Travels with Charley, Steinbeck

Treasure Island, Stevenson

A Tree Grows in Brooklyn, Smith

Tuck Everlasting, Babbitt/
    Bridge to Terabithia, Paterson

The Turn of the Screw/Daisy Miller,
    James

Uncle Tom's Cabin, Stowe

Walk Two Moons, Creech

Walkabout, Marshall

Watership Down, Adams

When the Legends Die, Borland

Where the Lilies Bloom, Cleaver/
    No Promises in the Wind, Hunt

Winesburg, Ohio, Anderson

The Witch of Blackbird Pond, Speare/
    My Brother Sam Is Dead, Collier
    and Collier

A Wrinkle in Time, L'Engle/The Lion,
    the Witch and the Wardrobe, Lewis

Wuthering Heights, Brontë

The Yearling, Rawlings/
    The Red Pony, Steinbeck

Zlata's Diary, Filipović/
    The Lottery Rose, Hunt

Drama

Antigone, Sophocles

Arms and the Man/Saint Joan, Shaw

The Crucible, Miller

Cyrano de Bergerac, Rostand

Death of a Salesman, Miller

A Doll's House/Hedda Gabler, Ibsen

The Glass Menagerie, Williams

The Importance of Being Earnest,
    Wilde

Inherit the Wind, Lawrence and Lee

Long Day's Journey into Night, O'Neill

A Man for All Seasons, Bolt

Medea, Euripides/The Lion in Winter,
    Goldman

The Miracle Worker, Gibson

Murder in the Cathedral, Eliot/Galileo,
    Brecht

The Night Thoreau Spent in Jail,
    Lawrence and Lee

Oedipus the King, Sophocles

Our Town, Wilder

The Playboy of the Western World/
    Riders to the Sea, Synge

Pygmalion, Shaw

A Raisin in the Sun, Hansberry

1776, Stone and Edwards

She Stoops to Conquer, Goldsmith/
    The Matchmaker, Wilder

A Streetcar Named Desire, Williams

Tartuffe, Molière

Three Comedies of American Family
    Life: I Remember Mama, van
    Druten/Life with Father, Lindsay
    and Crouse/You Can't Take It with
    You, Hart and Kaufman

Waiting for Godot, Beckett/
    Rosencrantz & Guildenstern Are
    Dead, Stoppard

Shakespeare

As You Like It

Hamlet

Henry IV, Part I

Henry V

Julius Caesar

King Lear

Macbeth

The Merchant of Venice

A Midsummer Night's Dream

Othello

Richard III

Romeo and Juliet

The Taming of the Shrew

The Tempest

Twelfth Night

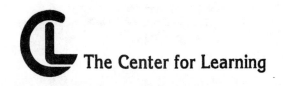

The Center for Learning

To Order Contact: **The Center for Learning—Shipping/Business Office**
P.O. Box 910 • Villa Maria, PA 16155
800-767-9090 • 412-964-8083 • Fax 888-767-8080

THE PUBLISHER

All instructional materials identified by the TAP® (Teachers/Authors/Publishers) trademark are developed by a national network of teachers whose collective educational experience distinguishes the publishing objective of The Center for Learning, a non-profit educational corporation founded in 1970.

Concentrating on values-related disciplines, The Center publishes humanities and religion curriculum units for use in public and private schools and other educational settings. Over 400 language arts, social studies, novel/drama, life issues, and faith publications are available.

While acutely aware of the challenges and uncertain solutions to growing educational problems, The Center is committed to quality curriculum development and to the expansion of learning opportunities for all students. Publications are regularly evaluated and updated to meet the changing and diverse needs of teachers and students. Teachers may offer suggestions for development of new publications or revisions of existing titles by contacting

The Center for Learning

Administrative/Editorial Office
21590 Center Ridge Road
Rocky River, Ohio, 44116
(216) 331-1404 • FAX (216) 331-5414
E-mail: cfl@stratos.net
Web: http://www.centerforlearning.org

For a free catalog, containing order and price information, and a descriptive listing of titles, contact

The Center for Learning

Shipping/Business Office
P.O. Box 910
Villa Maria, PA 16155
(412) 964-8083 • (800) 767-9090
FAX (888) 767-8080

Educator's Evaluation

The Center for Learning concept calls for frequent updates and revisions. Teachers writing for teachers will give us the best in instructional material.

Book Title_____

Excellent	Good	Fair	Poor	Criteria
				Overall effectiveness of the book
				Usability of the book
				Pacing of the material
				Quality of format and layout
				Availability of the selected text materials
				Student evaluation of the material
				Student motivation and interest
				Ability level of students
				Student achievement in the Unit

Used in Grade(s)_____

Used for
❏ Basic/Core for instruction
❏ Selected use
❏ Supplemental use

Teacher's experience
❏ 0-5 years
❏ 6-10 years
❏ 11-15 years
❏ 16 or more years

School Location
❏ large city
❏ suburb
❏ small town
❏ country

School Enrollment
❏ 1-499 students
❏ 500-999 students
❏ 1000 or more students

What is the greatest strength of this book?

What would you change in this book?

Additional Comments:

Name_____

Position _____

School _____

Address _____

Please return to:

The Center for Learning
21590 Center Ridge Rd.
Rocky River, Ohio 44116